fun with the family
New Jersey

Help Us Keep This Guide Up to Date

We would love to hear from you concerning your experiences with this guide and how you feel it could be improved and kept up to date. Please send your comments and suggestions to:

editorial@GlobePequot.com

Thanks for your input, and happy travels!

fun with the family
New Jersey

hundreds of ideas for day trips with the kids

First Edition

Francesca Di Meglio

travel

Guilford, Connecticut

All the information in this guidebook is subject to change. We recommend that you call ahead to obtain current information before traveling.

To buy books in quantity for corporate use or incentives, call **(800) 962-0973** or e-mail **premiums@GlobePequot.com.**

Editor: Amy Lyons
Project Editor: Heather Santiago
Layout: Joanna Beyer
Text design: Nancy Freeborn and Linda R. Loiewski
Maps © Morris Book Publishing, LLC
Spot photography throughout © Photodisc and © RubberBall Productions

ISBN 978-0-7627-5717-6

Printed in the United States of America
10 9 8 7 6 5 4 3 2 1

Contents

About the Author

Francesca Di Meglio is a freelance writer and editor in her hometown of Fort Lee, NJ. Born in neighboring Englewood, NJ, she has lived in the Garden State her entire life and considers her title as a Jersey Girl an honor. With a BA in journalism from the George Washington University in Washington, DC, Di Meglio has written for numerous publications and websites, including Monster.com, BusinessWeek, and iVillage. As the assistant travel editor at *Ladies' Home Journal* in New York City, she visited and wrote about Atlantic City, Boston, Philadelphia, and Disneyland Paris. On various road trips with her family and friends over the years, Di Meglio has seen much of her own great state and is happy to share her adventures with the readers of her personal website and blog, *Two Worlds*, at francescadimeglio.com. She writes the "Guide to Newlyweds" for About.com and regularly contributes to *Bloomberg Businessweek*, where she's a reporter covering management education. In true jet-setter fashion, she spends a lot of time in Italy with her husband, Antonio, and their son, Enzo.

Northern New Jersey

Central New Jersey

Southern New Jersey

Delaware Bay

Atlantic Ocean

Introduction

Home to the Lenni Lenape Indians starting about 10,000 years ago, New Jersey has a soulful history and rustic charm that often goes unnoticed by outsiders. Back when the small Lenape families lived together on the land, the men would hunt or fish for clams on the Jersey shore, while the women worked the gardens tending to vegetables, such as squash, sweet potatoes, and maize. In 1604, Henry Hudson claimed the land, which he named New Netherlands, for the Dutch, who lost it all to the British in 1664. Having played a vital role in the Revolutionary War with 100 battles waged on its land, including the legendary Battle of Trenton, New Jersey was the third state to ratify the US Constitution in 1787 and the first to sign the Bill of Rights (1789). Today the legacy of the state's first settlers lives on in the state's corn, which is still the sweetest you will ever taste, and its shore, which produces great riches every summer. And its eight million residents are as feisty as the colonials who fought for freedom and ultimately beat the British at their own game.

This book is broken down by county, from the northern part of the state neighboring Manhattan to the southern end, adjacent to Philadelphia. While each county is distinct in its own right, each borrows a bit from the cities that touch it, and you'll notice those influences throughout the book. Each entry includes an address, telephone number, website (if available), and description. Where possible, hours, prices, and directions have been added to the entry. Things change from time to time, so you should call ahead to confirm operating hours and prices. While there are suggested age ranges, you know your child best and can determine whether a site is appropriate for him or her.

Exploration of New Jersey—from its rich history to its lush land—can serve as an engaging education for both your children and you. But traveling with kids requires some planning on the part of parents. Maps at the start of each chapter can act as a guide for you, but they should not replace more complete maps you can use for charting your travels and finding your way.

New Jersey has evolved in many ways since the Lenape dominated. While famous New Jerseyans—from Bruce Springsteen to Jon Bon Jovi—have literally sung the state's praises, there have been many others giving New Jersey a bad rap. Woody Allen has referred to the state as a "primitive wasteland," and Andy Warhol suggested that the New Jersey state bird was a mosquito. Then, there's all that Gym Tan Laundry (GTL) nonsense and negative references to the state's large Italian-American population. You will forget all that as you travel through New Jersey. Take note of the sparkling George Washington Bridge in the evening or the soft sand between your toes as you walk on Sandy Hook's beach or the majesty of the pumpkin patches at one of Jersey's farms or the ringing of Atlantic City's slot machines. Share the wonders of a state that few know to treasure or love with your kids—and see for yourself how wild and brilliant New Jersey really is.

ATTRACTION, RESTAURANT & ACCOMMODATION FEES

In the "Where to Eat" and "Where to Stay" sections, dollar signs indicate general price ranges. For meals, the prices are for individual adult entrees. For accommodations, the rates are for a double room, for a family of four, with no meals, unless otherwise indicated; rates for lodging may be higher during peak vacation seasons and holidays. Always inquire about family and group rates and package deals that may include amusement park tickets, discounts for area attractions, and tickets for concerts and other performing arts events.

Because admission fees change frequently, this book offers a general idea of the prices charged by each attraction.

Rates for Attractions

$	less than $5
$$	$5 to $10
$$$	$10 to $20
$$$$	more than $20

Rates for Accommodations

$	less than $100
$$	$100 to $150
$$$	$150 to $200
$$$$	more than $200

Rates for Restaurants

$	most entrees under $10
$$	$10 to $15
$$$	$15 to $20
$$$$	most more than $20

Attractions Key

The following is a key to the icons found throughout the text.

SWIMMING	LODGING
BOATING/BOAT TOUR	CAMPING
HISTORIC SITE	MUSEUM
HIKING / WALKING	PERFORMING ARTS
FISHING	SPORTS/ATHLETICS
BIKING	PICNICKING
AMUSEMENT PARK	PLAYGROUND
HORSEBACK RIDING	SHOPPING
SKIING/WINTER SPORTS	PLANTS / GARDENS / NATURE TRAILS
PARK	FARM
ANIMAL VIEWING	HANDS-ON/CRAFTS
FOOD	

Northern New Jersey

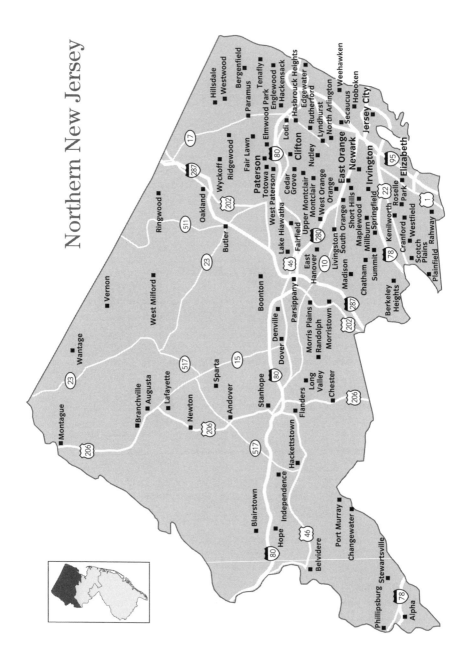

Northern
New Jersey

Passaic County

P assaic County, with a population of 501,226, is in the upper northeastern portion of New Jersey, and it has a dual personality. It is both industrial mecca and nature lover's paradise. Having an extraordinary history, the county dates back to 1837; its name has Native American origins and means "valley." The 16 towns that make up Passaic County include Clifton, Pompton Lakes, Wayne, Little Falls, Ringwood, and West Milford. The county's largest city and its seat, Paterson, is home to the Great Falls, which was recently named a national historic park. If you and your family want to learn about New Jersey's role in industry while still enjoying parks and fresh air, then Passaic County should be on your itinerary.

Clifton Arts Center and Sculpture Park (all ages)
Clifton Municipal Complex, 900 Clifton Ave., Clifton; (973) 472-5499; cliftonnj.org/content/clifton-arts-center-and-sculpture-park.html. Open year-round, but you should check the calendar because it is closed between art shows. $.
The Clifton Arts Center is special not only for its contents but also for its home. Housed in barns built in the early 20th century that were once the US Animal Quarantine Station, it is listed on the National Register of Historic Places. Today, the 2 barns are attached by an atrium. The Clifton Arts Center offers visitors the chance to check out visual arts exhibits. There are 6 art shows per year that each last 6 weeks. Professional artists, high school students, and even doctors have shared their work at the center. Sometimes, the center hosts fund-raisers, which have included a jazz concert, opera performance, and meet-and-greet with a book author. In the summer, children can partake in a 1-week arts camp. There

are sometimes art workshops, too. The highlight of the sculpture garden, which showcases the work of 30 contemporary sculptors, is the *One City One Nation* piece, which is a hallmark of Clifton because it honors the city's identity as a melting pot.

Garret Mountain Reservation (all ages)

311 Pennsylvania Ave., Paterson; (973) 881-4832; passaiccountynj.org. Open year-round from sunrise to sunset. Admission is free.

Located 500 feet above sea level, Garret Mountain Reservation might be most notable for the views of New York City and northern New Jersey that visitors can take in. You can hike, ride horses (there's an equestrian center), play sports (there's a cricket field and basketball court), fish, picnic, or cross-country ski. There's also a veteran's memorial on-site.

The highlight of Garret Mountain Reservation, however, is **Lambert Castle,** home of Catholina Lambert, a Brit who worked the mills in England and moved to the US for a shot at the American dream. While here, Lambert got into the silk business and ran the successful Dexter, Lambert and Company. He also married a socialite and indeed reached his goals. He had Lambert Castle built in Paterson to fulfill a childhood fantasy he had about having a home like the castles he would pass in England on his way to the mills. Although the Lamberts faced tragedies—many children who passed away and bankruptcy at the end of Catholina's life—the castle remained in the family until Catholina passed away. Then his son sold it to the city, which gathered historical items that now fill the house. A visit to the house gives you the chance to learn about the silk industry's past and the history of Paterson. Although the grounds are open everyday, the museum is open only Wed through Sun from noon to 4 p.m.

The castle isn't the only exciting site to see on the reservation. At **Rifle Camp Park,** families enjoy what has been called "the best view of New York City in the world." A small nature museum and observatory are highlights. Nature trails and picnic areas round out the park's offerings. Word is that you are sure to spot a deer or two feeding in the meadow.

Great Falls Park (all ages)

McBride Avenue Extension and Spruce Street, Paterson; (973) 279-9587; nps.gov/pagr. Open year-round. Free to the public.

The city of Paterson is known as the "cradle of American industry," largely thanks to the Great Falls, a 77-foot waterfall that is the second largest on the East Coast and among the largest in the US. The falls once provided power that helped launch the American Industrial Revolution. Without the Great Falls, in fact, Paterson might not have even existed.

In the late 1700s, Alexander Hamilton, secretary of the Treasury, developed plans to create the Society for Establishing Useful Manufacturing (SUM). The directors of SUM founded Paterson, which was named after then New Jersey governor William Paterson to thank him for giving the green light to their business plans, at the Great Falls. The waterfall would be used to deliver power through a three-tiered raceway system. Companies that produced textile

A State **for All Seasons**

Whatever the weather, you can find something fun to do in New Jersey—yes, even when the snow is falling.

In the **winter,** you can take advantage of the skiing, snowboarding, and sledding available at places such as **Mountain Creek** (p. 14) in Vernon. Even if you're not one for staying out in the cold, you can curl up in the lodge with a hot chocolate and a smile.

When nature comes out of hibernation in the **spring,** you can hike one of New Jersey's many historic parks. From the **Great Falls** (p. 3) in Paterson to **Princeton Battlefield State Park** (p. 74), there is natural beauty to admire and history to learn.

The **summer** means going "down the shore" and taking advantage of the Atlantic Ocean beaches on the state's coast and hanging out on the boardwalk at your beach of choice. Visit **Lucy the Elephant** (p. 139) in Margate or take a ride on the Ferris wheel at the **Steel Pier** (p. 135) in Atlantic City, or visit the fish at **Jenkinson's Aquarium** (p. 102) in Point Pleasant Beach.

When the leaves turn color in the **fall,** New Jersey is perhaps at its finest. The Garden State's farms pick up the pace at the farmers' markets with the autumn harvest and give visitors the opportunity to pick their own apples and pumpkins. As if that weren't enough, many of these same events offer hayrides and corn mazes to boot.

machinery, steam locomotives, silk weaving and dyeing, revolvers, and aircraft engines popped up in the area. Although SUM failed to meet its manufacturing goals, it continued to exist into the 20th century.

Recently, President Barack Obama declared Great Falls a national historic park. This means the 35-acre site is eligible for federal funds, which will be used to further develop the area. The goal is for the new and improved park, combined with the majestic beauty of the falls, to spark interest in tourism and revitalize the city. The Great Falls site is a natural wonder with historical significance, which is a rare treasure hidden in Paterson.

Long Pond Ironworks State Park
(ages 6 and up)

1334 Greenwood Lake Tpke., West Milford; (973) 657-1688; longpondironworks .org. Open year-round from 8 a.m. to 8 p.m., with the museum open on weekends Apr through Nov from 1 to 4 p.m. Monthly walking tours feature a suggested donation of $3. Otherwise, admission is free.

The Long Pond Ironworks State Park is a work in progress. Renovation projects are underway, but Hurricane Irene damaged the area in 2011. Still, there is something for families to see if they visit. One waterwheel has been reconstructed. With the Wanaque River as a backdrop, the old stone walls and furnaces, dating to the 18th and 19th centuries, serve as reminders of the once-industrious zone. Founded in 1766 by German ironmaster Peter Hasenclever, Long Pond Ironworks closed in 1882. The ironworks village that remains a testament to history produced iron for the Continental Army, the American soldiers fighting the War of 1812, and the Union Army during the Civil War. To get charcoal for the furnaces, the ironworks leaders cut down forests, and to get hydropower, they diverted the river. But today the remnants of these industry titans stand next to flourishing forests that have grown back and the flowing river.

Diner **Heaven**

New Jersey has more diners than any other state in the country, and it is considered the "Diner Capital of the World," according to the History Channel. Indeed, just about every town in Jersey has its own diner, a hangout where all the cool kids go after football games, twentysomethings retreat after nights out on the town, and seniors gather for lunch with their pals. Many of the state's diners are open 24 hours, and they offer large menus full of affordable dishes, usually including french fries in gravy, waffles, pies, salads, burgers, and milk shakes—and you can order whatever you'd like any time of day. If you and your family want to experience an authentic New Jersey diner, you might consider feasting at one of the following:

Mustache Bill's Diner, 8th St., Barnegat Light; (609) 494-0155. Old-fashioned fare, including chipped beef and BLTs, have made this diner an institution with locals. Being featured on Food Network, however, has made the weekend lines incredibly long, so be prepared.

Skylark Diner, 17 Wooding Ave., Edison; (732) 777-7878; skylark diner.com. Its retro look is as inviting as its menu, which includes more refined diner offerings, such as homemade mozzarella triangles and au poivre burger, which features a black pepper–crusted burger, wild mushrooms, an au poivre sauce, and malt vinegar fries. Rated among the best diners in New Jersey by *Zagat*, it's a popular choice with locals and visitors alike.

Tick Tock Diner, 281 Allwood Rd., Clifton; (973) 777-0511; thetick tockdiner.com. Originally built in 1948, the Tick Tock Diner, although restored over the years, remains an art deco building with chrome and enamel exterior. Hickory-smoked spare ribs are among the diner's specialties, as is the Rich and Sassy Sauce, which is made from a secret recipe that you'll long to know.

White Manna Hamburgers, 358 River St., Hackensack; (201) 342-0914. Inside a tiny shack in Hackensack, the Bergen County seat, you'll find some of the best sliders you've ever eaten. At lunch, you can barely get into the very small diner, but it is worth the crowds. This place is such a legend that a photo of it hangs in one of the Disneyland Paris hotels.

Ritz Diner, 72 E. Mount Pleasant Ave., Livingston; (973) 533-1213. The matzo ball soup and apple pie are considered must-haves, and some have given great reviews to the french fries smothered in mozzarella and gravy.

Hightstown Diner, 151 Mercer St., Hightstown; (609) 443-4600. Large portions and the sense that everyone knows your name make this joint popular even with tourists trying to escape the Turnpike for a little while.

Jefferson Diner, 5 Bowling Green Pkwy., Lake Hopatcong; (973) 663-0233; jeffersondiner.com. Another shiny diner, replete with enamel and chrome exterior, this diner serves classic diner food and what it claims to be the largest club sandwiches in the state. Quite popular, this diner was featured on a couple of Food Network shows and other programs, such as *Good Morning America.*

Brownstone Diner & Pancake Factory, 426 Jersey Ave., Jersey City; (201) 433-0471; brownstonediner.com. Chosen by *New Jersey Monthly* magazine as the best place for pancakes in the state, the Brownstone Diner & Pancake Factory serves 30 kinds of pancakes and pancake wraps, which are pancakes stuffed with other breakfast items. The Original Pancake Wrap, for instance, is an oversize pancake brimming with scrambled eggs, bacon, and American cheese.

Tops Diner, 500 Passaic Ave., East Newark; (973) 481-0490; thetops diner.com. Tops, like many diners, serves up a bit of everything—from burgers and pizzas to eggs and pancakes. Specialty drinks are a unique offering that some diners forego.

Paterson Museum (ages 7 and up)

Thomas Rogers Locomotive Manufacturing Building, 2 Market St., Paterson; (973) 279-9587; patersonmuseum.com. Open Tues through Fri from 10 a.m. to 4 p.m. and Sat and Sun from 12:30 to 4:30 p.m. Adults $2, children are free.
Organized in 1925, the Paterson Museum began as a library exhibit that showcased items donated by townspeople. Over the years, the collection has grown to fill a full-fledged museum. Visitors can learn about local archaeology, history, and mineralogy. Most of all, they can educate themselves about the city's role in various industries. The museum features exhibits on silk weaving and dyeing, trains and locomotives, Colt firearms, and Holland submarines. Located 1 block east of the Great Falls, the museum can be part of a longer day trip in Paterson.

Ringwood State Park (all ages)

1304 Sloatsburg Rd., Ringwood; (973) 962-2240; nj.gov/dep/parksandforests. Open year-round between 8 a.m. and 8 p.m. Shepherd Lake is open but swimming and boating is only available from Memorial Day to Labor Day. Parking fees apply to the different areas of the park from Memorial Day to Labor Day and sometimes vary, depending on whether it is the weekend or a weekday, free the rest of the year. $$.
Ringwood State Park offers a wide range of activities for families. From Memorial Day to Labor Day, you can swim, boat, canoe, and fish at **Shepherd Lake Recreation Area.** Boat rentals are available. There are lovely trails nearby that lead to rocky vistas for you and your family to admire. And it serves as the perfect summer destination, a place to cool off, lie back, relax, and enjoy nature.

Devotion to Mother Nature can continue at the nearby New Jersey Botanical Gardens, which is part of the Tudor Revival mansion, **Skylands Manor,** built for Clarence McKenzie Lewis by renowned architect John Russell Pope in the early 20th century. The mansion features antique stained glass set in leaded windows and a spiral staircase rail. The **New Jersey Botanical Gardens** are an extension of the beauty and elegance of the mansion. There, visitors can pass through the Annual Garden, which changes according to the season, Crab Apple Allée, which is considered the highlight of the grounds with its profusion of pink blossoms come May, and Magnolia Walk, which is interesting because these typically Southern plants thrive here. Little ones might appreciate the Octagonal Garden for its many dwarf plants, which are close to their own size. In addition to the flowers, the botanical garden offers arts and crafts opportunities for families.

To round out your time at Ringwood State Park, you can visit **Ringwood Manor,** a mansion that was home to a succession of ironmasters for nearly 200 years. Unlike Skylands Manor, Ringwood Manor had many inhabitants who all put their own stamp on the home. The house is considered more casual and less regal than most, but it teaches lessons about the people who lived there and the iron industry in New Jersey. Call ahead to find out when tours are available and about events, such as Victorian Christmas, an annual attraction at the manor that has guides dressed in period costume taking visitors from room to room to see authentic 19th-century Christmas decor during the holiday season.

Yogi Berra Museum & Learning Center (all ages)

Montclair State University, 8 Yogi Berra Dr., Little Falls; (973) 655-2378; yogiberra museum.org. Open year-round, Wed through Sun from noon to 5 p.m. $–$$. Located next door to **Yogi Berra Stadium,** which is home to the minor-league New Jersey Jackals and Montclair State Red Hawks, the Yogi Berra Museum & Learning Center was established in 1998 by admirers of the retired New York Yankees star. Fans of the Yankees and baseball in general will appreciate the memorabilia, which includes Berra's 10 world championship rings. A theater that looks like a ballpark engages visitors in films during museum hours and serves as a classroom and venue for public programs. In fact, you should call ahead to find out if the museum is closed for a private event. Children can even host their birthday parties at the museum. With a little planning, you could take in both a baseball game and the museum in a day. Sounds like a baseball fan's dream.

Where to Eat

Akcafe. 415 Crooks Ave., Clifton; (973) 340-0060; akcafe.com. Open everyday for breakfast, lunch, and dinner. Kid friendly, Akcafe provides Turkish dishes at affordable prices. $–$$

Burger Deluxe. 1420 Rte. 23 North, Wayne; (973) 305-0033; theburgerdeluxe.com. Open Sun through Thurs from 11 a.m. to 10 p.m., and Fri and Sat from 11 a.m. to 11 p.m. Burgers and milk shakes reign supreme at this retro chic diner with countertop dining that will have you feel like you journeyed back to the '50s. $

The Village Inn. 422 Runnymede Dr., Wayne; (973) 696-0555; thevillageinnofwayne .com. Open Tues through Sun from 5 to 10 p.m. and Fri and Sat from 5 to 11 p.m. From the baked brie en croute to the banana cheesecake spring roll, the Village Inn fills your belly with love. $$

Where to Stay

Holiday Inn Express. 303 Union Ave., Haskell-Wayne; (973) 839-4405; hiexpress .com. The quiet Twin Lakes setting will help you and your family relax. $$

La Quinta Inn & Suites. 1850 Rte. 23 North, Wayne; (973) 696-8050; lq.com. Being able to bring your pets and do your laundry are pluses. $

Residence Inn Wayne. 30 Nevins Rd., Wayne; (973) 872-7100; marriott.com/ Wayne. Complimentary breakfast and hospitality hour in the evenings are nice touches. $$$

Sussex County

I n the northwest corner of the state lies Sussex County, which is strategically located because it borders Pennsylvania to the west and New York to the east. Part of the Skylands, the region of northwest New Jersey that includes Morris, Somerset, Hunterdon, and Warren Counties, Sussex plays an important role in the state's tourism. The natural beauty of Sussex County—with its rich agriculture and miles of wilderness—might be the reason New Jersey earned its moniker as the Garden State. In fact, about one-third of the county's 521 square miles is made up of state parks and forest areas. Despite being a natural wonderland, its proximity to major cities in New Jersey, New York, and Pennsylvania attracts many a visitor. With a population of 149,265, Sussex County might feel as though everyone knows your name, which makes for a welcoming and cozy getaway.

Appalachian Trail (all ages)
High Point State Park to the Delaware Water Gap; njskylands.com/odhikeaptrl .htm. Open year-round. Admission is free for all.
Want to get a feel for what life was like 200 years ago? Then you won't want to miss the Appalachian Trail, which extends from Georgia to Maine and includes about 42 miles in New Jersey. The majority of the trail is undeveloped, and the few visible towns along it remain rural. Passing through High Point State Park and the Delaware Water Gap, you and your family can opt to take a short walk on the trail as opposed to covering the whole thing, which is reserved for serious hikers and can be too challenging for families with young children. If you decide to take to the trail, you should dress everyone in long-sleeve shirts and long

pants to protect against deer ticks. To locate the exact points of the trail, you should pick up a good road map of New Jersey or check with the forest ranger offices at one of the nearby parks.

Once you've taken the necessary precautions and chosen your route, you can indulge in the natural treasures of the trail. The views of the Kittatinny Mountains are exceptional. And bird lovers will observe plenty of hawks, eagles, and towhee. You might also spot a bear or a rattlesnake, so be careful.

Delaware Water Gap National Recreation Area (all ages)

1 Broad St., Delaware Water Gap, PA; (570) 426-2452; nps.gov/dewa. **Grounds open daily during daylight hours; visitor center closed in winter. Entrance is free, but some amenities require a fee.**

The 67,000 acres of the Delaware Water Gap National Recreation Area are loaded with educational lessons that cover both science and history. The park itself encompasses the river valley in two states (New Jersey and Pennsylvania, thus the address) and includes the Middle Delaware River itself. In addition to exploring the Appalachian Trail that runs through it, visitors can fish, camp, canoe, kayak, raft, tube, and picnic. They can also observe the land's historical significance, including Native American archaeological sites and the remnants of the early Dutch settlers. In fact, intact 18th- and 19th-century rural villages remain on the Jersey side. Kids can also check out their own dedicated page on the website and aim to earn a patch in the park's junior ranger program.

Franklin Mineral Museum (all ages)

32 Evans St., Franklin; (973) 827-3481; franklinmineralmuseum.com. **Open weekends Mar through Nov. Open daily Apr through Nov, Mon through Fri from 10 a.m. to 4 p.m., Sat from 10 a.m. to 5 p.m., and Sun from 11 a.m. to 5 p.m. Admission to museum exhibits costs $7 for adults, $4 for children ages 3 to 12, and $5 for seniors; rock collecting costs $7 for adults, $4 for children ages 3 to 12, and $5 for seniors; to visit the museum and go rock collecting costs $12 for adults, $7 for children ages 3 to 12, and $8 for seniors.**

As the "fluorescent mineral capital of the world," Franklin, along with Ogdensburg, NJ, is the home of the most famous zinc mines. With over 4,000 mineral specimens on display, curators call this museum "nature's classroom." Kids and adults alike get a kick out of the fluorescent room, where fluorescent minerals and their rainbow of glowing colors light up the space. The mine replica shows visitors the methods that miners in Franklin used. A collection of Native American tools and artifacts; plant, marine, and wildlife fossils; a petrified wood display; and more minerals round out the museum's offerings.

Heaven Hill Farm (all ages)

451 Rte. 94, Vernon; (973) 764-5144; heavenhillfarm.com. Open year-round but offerings change with the season. Prices vary depending on activities and attractions.

While Heaven Hill Farm has activities for every season (Santa even visits the farm ahead of Christmas), it is most active in the fall. The **Pumpkinland Festival,** which runs from Sept through Oct, has guests picking their own pumpkins, enjoying pig races, a hay maze, and visiting farm animals. For additional fees, you can also partake in carnival rides, pony rides, and face painting. Slightly older children who don't spook easily can sign up for the Haunted Acres Hayride, which features lots of frightening sites, including whatever is hiding in the cornfields and psychotic clowns. The Boo Barn and a Halloween-costume shop round out the activities until the season-ending Pumpkin Palooza, aimed at destroying leftover and rotten pumpkins. The day's activities include impaling pumpkins on dart boards, using them as bowling balls, and dropping your pumpkin from a giant boom lift. Champion eaters can try their hands—err, their stomachs—in the pumpkin-pie-eating contest for a chance to win prizes.

High Point State Park (all ages)

1480 Rte. 23, Sussex; (973) 875-4800; state.nj.us/dep/parksandforests. Open daily from 8 a.m. to 4:30 p.m. Park office open daily from 9 a.m. to 4 p.m. Entrance fees are charged per vehicle from Memorial Day weekend to Labor Day, $5 on weekdays and $10 on weekends.

This 15,827-acre state park offers a little bit of everything in every season. In warmer weather, you will enjoy swimming, boat launching, picknicking, fishing, hiking (the Appalachian Trail), and camping. When the temperature drops and the snow arrives, you can partake in cross-country skiing, snowmobiling, snowshoeing, and ice-skating.

As if that weren't enough, High Point State Park gets its name from being home of the Kitatinny Mountain Ridge, which includes the highest point in New Jersey at 1,803 feet above sea level. Still,

the highlight of the park is the **High Point Monument,** which was built thanks to a donation by the Kuser family and is meant to honor war veterans. Those who venture to the top of the monument will take in breathtaking views of the Pocono Mountains, Catskill Mountains, and Wallkill River Valley.

Mountain Creek Mountain (all ages)

200 Rte. 94, Vernon; (973) 827-2000; mountaincreek.com. Open in winter Mon through Thurs from 9 a.m. to 9 p.m., Fri and Sat from 9 a.m. to 10 p.m., and Sun from 9 a.m. to 9 p.m. Prices vary depending on age and mountain.

Once known as Vernon Valley/Great Gorge, Mountain Creek has been attracting skiers and snowboarders for quite some time. The resort boasts 4 peaks with 2 distinct areas. Families will be drawn to Vernon Peak, which is best for alpine skiing and riding, downhill skiing, and beginners with little to no experience. Here, you can get lessons, rent equipment, or go snow tubing. Those with more experience can visit the intermediate terrain. And the high-speed gondola is practical and fun. South Base is for those interested in freestyle skiing and snowboarding and indulging in the resort's social scene. There are four high-quality resorts—Grand Cascades Lodge, Minerals Resort & Spa, The Appalachian, and Black Creek Sanctuary—at which you can stay within the Crystal Springs Resort (see p. 18). Kids will enjoy planning their trip on the kids-oriented page on the resort's website. With all there is for adults and kids at the resort, no one will be left out in the cold.

Mountain Creek Waterpark (ages 2 and up)

200 Rte. 94, Vernon; (973) 864-8444; mountaincreekwaterpark.com. Open in the summer. Season passes for one cost of $59.99, and season parking passes cost $16.99.

Mountain Creek continues to deliver in the summer, when the resort's water park, with two dozen rides and attractions, opens. Although the park highlights many thrill rides that are better suited for older kids and adults, you'll have to coax the kids out of the attractions aimed at them. The Fishing Village is a multilevel fort that features waterslides, spray cannons, water hoses, and 2 waterfalls. There are tube rides specifically designed for guests under 48 inches tall and their guardians. A body slide that glides little ones from a waterfall to a cover near a wave pool might be your child's favorite part of the day. A frog slide and whale fountains in a play area suited to toddlers

Kids' **Reads**

Get your kids in the spirit for a trip to New Jersey by having them read one of the many children's books about the state. Here are a few you might share with them:

G is for Garden State: A New Jersey Alphabet (Sleeping Bear Press, 2004): An exploration of the state's people, places, and things, the book is designed to teach the letters of the alphabet.

Good Night New Jersey (Our World of Books, 2008): Discover the iconic attractions of New Jersey while putting your kids to bed for the night.

State Shapes New Jersey (Black Dog & Leventhal Publishers, 2010): In the shape of the Garden State, this book covers the history, geography, and people of New Jersey and includes fun facts on the Appalachian Trail, Princeton University, and more.

The New Jersey Colony (Capstone Press, 2006): Find out what the Garden State was like—including its government and economy—back when it was a colony.

My First Book about New Jersey (Gallopade Intl, 2000): Kids will enjoy learning about the state bird, motto, flower, etc., as well as New Jersey's history. It's also chock-full of activities that help teach basic state facts.

will delight even the littlest among your family. And you will all enjoy being lazy and lounging in tubes on the Lost Island River. Thrill seekers in the family will appreciate some of the newer additions to Mountain Creek, including zip lines, which have you gliding across the sky from as high as 200 feet above the ground, and the Alpine Mountain Coaster, which is described as a "cross between an alpine slide and a twisting roller coaster" on the Mountain Creek website.

Space Farms Zoo & Museum (all ages)

218 Rte. 519, Sussex; (973) 875-5800; spacefarms.com. Open daily from Apr through Oct. from 9 a.m. to 5 p.m. $$$; children under 3 free.

"Lions, tigers, and bears, oh my," is what you might find yourself shouting when you visit Space Farms Zoo & Museum, which is home to more than 500 animals, including everything from your basic goats and pigs to Himalayan bears, tigers, and lions. The 11 museum buildings house antiques, classic cars, toys, Native American artifacts, and more. The quaint zoo and museum also offer a playground and picnic area, perfect for families.

Sterling Hill Mining Museum (ages 7 and up)

30 Plant St., Ogdensburg; (973) 209-MINE; sterlinghillminingmuseum.org. Check website for hours because they change by season. Tour costs $10 for adults, $9 for seniors, and $8 for children ages 12 and under.

This museum, previously serving as the Sterling Hill zinc mine, was once the real deal. Today visitors can learn as much about the minerals found on-site as they can the life of the miners who worked there. Throughout the grounds, you will encounter equipment that was once used in mining the area, including

sinking buckets, items used for explosives and moving and crushing ore, drum hoists, and more. One of the highlights is the 1,300-foot underground walking tour through the actual mine. For those who are concerned, you will walk on hard-pressed gravel, and there is no climbing involved. In fact, the whole tour is wheelchair accessible.

Along the way, you view not only the equipment miners used but also the lamp room, shaft station, and mine galleries dating to the 1830s. This leads up to the Rainbow Room, where the walls glow bright green and red, thanks to the exposed fluorescent zinc ore minerals. Kids will love the fact that they are encouraged to take a piece of the fluorescent zinc ore from the room as a souvenir. At the Rock Discovery Center, an outdoor area, children learn about the rocks that are quarried in the region, from slate to basalt, and can take home a sample of each type. And the Fossil Discovery Center has kids digging in a large sandbox for fossils to take home as souvenirs.

Sussex County Fairgrounds (all ages)

37 Plains Rd., Augusta; newjerseystatefair.org. Check online calendar for events and times. Prices vary.

August is the prime time to visit the Sussex County Fairgrounds because that is when the place comes alive for the New Jersey State Fair Sussex County Farm and Horse Show. A vegetable show, featuring the Garden State's finest, a flirtatious robot to entertain the crowd, musical entertainment, and livestock demonstrations are among the activities at the state fair. Of course, as the name implies, horse shows that include jumping and other special skills are part of the entertainment. On Sat from May through Oct (except during the week of the fair) from 9 a.m. to 2 p.m., Sussex County farmers sell their locally grown products, including vegetables, fruit, meat, cheese, honey, eggs, flowers, baked goods, wine, and more.

Where to Eat

Candy Apple Shoppe. 967 Rte. 517, Glenwood; (973) 764-4060; candy-apple-shoppe.com. Open Tues through Sat from noon to 6 p.m. and Sun from noon to 3 p.m. All sorts of caramel apples are the main draw at this sweets shop. $–$$

Krogh's Restaurant & Brew Pub. 23 White Deer Plaza, Sparta; (973) 729-8428; kroghs.com. Open every day for lunch and dinner. Offering crafted beer for the adults and everything from shrimp to ribs for everyone. Krogh's sometimes has live entertainment. $$$

Where to Stay

Econo Lodge Newton. 448 Rte. 206 South, Newton; (973) 383-3922; econolodge .com. A pet-friendly option, this hotel offers **free,** complimentary breakfast. $

Grand Cascades Lodge. Crystal Springs Resort, 3 Wild Turkey Way, Hamburg; (866) 599-6674; crystalgolfresort.com. A new Adirondack-style hotel, this place brings luxury to new levels replete with an indoor tropical-biosphere pool complex and a spa. $$$$

Quality Inn. 15 Rte. 94 and Route 23, Vernon; (973) 827-4666 or (866) 599-6674; qualityinn.com. This is a good option for those who are looking for affordable accommodations. $

Bergen County

O ne of four original New Jersey counties, Bergen County is 239 square miles of fun tucked into the northeast corner of the state. Thanks to its location near a major city, Bergen County, with Hackensack as its seat, is a melting pot that includes large populations of Latino and Korean Americans. In Bergen County's East Rutherford, you'll find the Meadowlands Sports Complex, home of Giants Stadium, where the New York Giants and Jets play, and host to a slew of events and concerts—including, every so often, New Jersey's finest, Bruce Springsteen and Bon Jovi. More than 900,000 people live in Bergen County, which is known for its vicinity to Manhattan but clearly boasts its own unique charms—from a small but sweet zoo to a jousting tournament replete with a falcon.

The Baylor Massacre Site (all ages)

River Vale Road and Red Oak Drive, River Vale; (201) 336-7267; co.bergen.nj.us/ bcparks. Free.

Walk the park of the Baylor Massacre Site in River Vale and you will relive a tragic moment in the American Revolution but learn a lot about bravery and history. Throughout the park you will find markers commemorating members of the Third Continental Light Dragoons. As many as 22 men died from wounds incurred by British forces on September 28, 1778. The next day the Bergen County Militia was sent to help survivors. They quickly buried the dead in abandoned leather tanning vats for fear that the British would return. What's even more interesting about this park is that it almost never was. If it wasn't for the work of a few interested people in the community, the site would have been lost forever in 1967, when construction was supposed to take place in the area. During an archaeological dig, experts located the remains of six dragoons. In 1974, the remains were reburied at the site, and the original tanning millstone was set as their gravestone. Today, you can learn the entire story on plaques along a walkway in the park.

Camp Merritt Memorial Monument (all ages)

Traffic Circle at Knickerbocker Road and Madison Avenue, Creskill; (201) 336-7267; co.bergen.nj.us/bcparks. Open year-round. Free to walk through.
More than one million soldiers passed through the embarkation camp in Creskill on their way to Europe to fight in World War I. Not many people knew about the camp because the government strove to keep the movement of the military under wraps. Named for Civil War officer Gen. Wesley Merritt, the 770-acre camp is long gone but not forgotten. In its place stands a 65-inch granite obelisk memorial modeled after Washington, DC's Washington Monument and featuring the names of the 578 people who died at the camp, mostly a result of the 1918 influenza epidemic. At the memorial site, visitors can take in a relief by Robert Ingersoll Aitkin of a doughboy with an eagle overhead, and another by Katherine Lamb Tait of the Palisades. There's also a map of Camp Merritt carved in stone, so you can see what once was.

Campgaw Mountain Reservation (all ages)

200 Campgaw Rd., Mahwah; (201) 327-7800; co.bergen.nj.us/bcparks. Open year-round but call ahead to determine hours for the activity of interest to you. Prices vary.
A playground for families, Campgaw offers opportunities to try your hand at archery, disc golf, skiing, snowboarding, and tubing in a wooded area. Novice skiers are welcome, and no experience is required for tubing. You can even sign up for skiing lessons for the little ones. If hiking is more your speed, you can take to the trails in the 1,373-acre park. You can even bring man's best friend.

New Jersey **in Song**

Even if some outsiders erroneously refer to New Jersey as the "Armpit of America" (you know who you are), many musicians know better. Over the years, a few singers have sung odes to the fair state that has inspired them:

"Jersey Girl" by Tom Waits

"Wildwood Days" by Bobby Rydell

"Fourth of July, Asbury Park (Sandy)" by Bruce Springsteen

"Who Says You Can't Go Home" by Bon Jovi

"I'm From New Jersey" by Red Mascara

"I Like Jersey Best" by J. Cosgriff and T. Bernardi

Easton Tower (all ages)

Red Mill Road, Route 4, and Saddle River Road, Paramus; (201) 336-7267; co.ber
gen.nj.us/bcparks. Visible year-round. **Free** to pass through it.

This unique structure was built around 1900 along the Saddle River as part of
a landscaped park. A stonemasonry tower topped with a wood structure, the
Easton Tower was used to pump water for irrigation. Once neighboring prosperous mills, the tower got its name from Edward D. Easton, who struck it rich as
the founder and president of the Columbia Phonograph Company, one of the
major recording companies at the turn of the 20th century.

Flat Rock Brook Nature Center (all ages)

443 Van Nostrand Ave., Englewood; (201) 567-1265; flatrockbrook.org. Check the
website or call to find out about special programs and events and their prices
and age ranges. Trails and picnic area are open year-round from dawn to dusk.
Free.

All that is left of the Palisades Forest, Flat Rock Brook Nature Center is a 150-
acre preserve and education center in Englewood. Established in 1973 by those

dedicated to land conservation, the land serves as a sanctuary for plant and animal life in the middle of an urban area. Your family will delight in observing everything from a wildflower meadow to the turtles and ducks in the pond. The little ones might also find having a picnic at Flat Rock amid nature fun. Just remember to respect the home of these animals and leave the faintest of footprints on your way out.

Fort Lee Historic Park (ages 7 and up)

Palisades Interstate Park, Hudson Terrace, Fort Lee; (201) 461-1776; njpalisades .org. Grounds open 8 a.m. to dusk; visitor center open Wed through Sun 10 a.m. to 4:45 p.m. Parking fee in season; $.

Located on a cliff-top bluff where the Continental Army positioned its batteries over the Hudson, Fort Lee Historic Park brings history alive and offers commanding views of the George Washington Bridge. On one end of the park, from two overlooks, visitors can take photos of the GWB and New York City skyline. If you're lucky enough to visit for a special holiday, such as Fourth of July, you might capture the bridge donning a large American flag or aglow with lights. When the weather is warmer, you can take in the scene and snack at one of the nearby picnic tables or benches.

In the middle of the park you will find the visitor center, which unlocks Fort Lee's history—specifically, the role the town played in the Revolutionary War. Much of the material recounts how George Washington and his soldiers were forced to leave the area in November 1776 for the famous "retreat to victory" across New Jersey. On the southern end of the park during weekends and summers when the weather permits, visitors can get a taste for 18th-century life. Actors in period costumes share the ways of that era. They might show you how to make traditional apple fritters or shoot a musket. Don't be surprised if you feel as though George Washington himself is present.

Garretson Forge & Farm (all ages)

4-02 River Rd., Fair Lawn; (551) 206-4380; co.bergen.nj.us/bcparks. Visible from dawn to sunset from the road or bikeway. Free.

One of the oldest sites in the county, Garretson Forge & Farm gives visitors the chance to go back in time and experience a life on an authentic Dutch farm. Your family can learn about restoration, preservation, and local history with actors dressed in traditional pre-Revolutionary garb. The garden is specially designed to attract butterflies. Many believe the house, a sandstone structure, was once home to an Indian encampment. The whole area provides great photo opportunities.

Gethsamene Cemetery (all ages)

Between Summit Place and Liberty Street, Little Ferry; (201) 336-7267; co.bergen .nj.us/bcparks. Call ahead for an appointment. Free.

Founded in 1860, this cemetery was designated as the burial ground for Hackensack's "colored population." A few important people are buried at the site, including Elizabeth Dulfer, a slave turned wealthy landowner, and Civil War veterans Peter Billings and Silas M. Carpenter. Visitors can learn about the cemetery's history, the role it played in getting the "Negro Burial Bill" passed (which said that businesses could not make a distinction between a black and white man, and therefore a black man could be buried where he chose), and the names of the more than 500 people buried there.

George Washington Bridge (all ages)

Fort Lee; panynj.gov. Open year-round. Tolls for drivers; free for walkers, runners, and cyclists; $–$$ (tolls).

The busiest bridge in the world, with 106 million vehicles per year passing through, the George Washington Bridge actually offers families an opportunity

Jersey's Main Man:
George Washington

Don't be surprised to see GEORGE WASHINGTON SLEPT HERE signs just about anywhere you go in this great state. The country's first president spent much of his time during the Revolutionary War in Jersey. He even won some of his most important battles here, namely the Battles of Trenton and Princeton. Throughout this book, you will discover places you can go that reveal what his life was like as he was birthing the nation—from the kinds of homes he used for shelter to the way he and his troop braved the long, hard winter. Of course, you'll also learn about the role New Jersey played in winning the Revolution. In fact, you could dedicate an entire family vacation to tracing GW's steps up and down the Garden State.

for some diversion and education. Considered a marvel of engineering in its day for its sleek look and ability to handle two tiers of vehicles, the George Washington Bridge, which was designed by Othmar Ammann, first opened to traffic in 1932. Of course, you can take your family for a drive over the bridge into Manhattan or one of New York's other boroughs, but that might cost you in the way of tolls. Instead, assuming the weather is permitting, you could walk, run, or bicycle across the bridge as a family. Spanning the Hudson River, you'll get to take in the views of both New York's skyline and New Jersey's scenic Palisades. The fresh air coming off the river is like no other, and it's sure to keep your kids awake and happy.

Hackensack Water Works Museum (all ages)
383 Kinderkamack Rd., Oradell; (201) 265-1000; hwwc.org/index.html. Call for schedule and pricing.

An architecturally and historically significant building, the Hackensack Water Works is a living timeline of technology with its intact steam pumping equipment. The Water Works Conservancy, in addition to advocating for the building's preservation, educates visitors and promotes the conservation of the Hackensack River and its role in the environment. Specifically, visitors to the museum, which is close to the original building, can see the steam pumping technology that was used in the early 20th century to provide a new water treatment and delivery process that purified the water and made it safe to drink. For the first time in history, the water was free from water-born diseases, and this is the process that became the international standard. A glimpse at the timeline of 100 years of the technology's evolution and temporary exhibits, such as "Glaciers to Suburbs," round out the museum's offerings. In addition to educating the public about the history of water treatment, the group that maintains the museum is also working to re-create the Hackensack River habitat on Van Buskirk Island, the site of the Hackensack Water Works.

Meadowlands Sports Complex (all ages)
50 Rte. 120, East Rutherford; (201) 935-8500; meadowlands.com. Open year-round; call for schedule and tickets to various events. Price varies, depending on the event you are attending; you pay for parking, too; $$–$$$$.

The Meadowlands Sports Complex offers all sorts of entertainment for families— from the circus to concerts, from football to horse racing. Covering 700 acres, the complex includes the Izod Center, the Meadowlands Racetrack, and MetLife Stadium, a brand new football stadium that is home to National Football League (NFL) teams the New York Giants and the New York Jets. That's right. Both "New York" teams actually play in New Jersey.

At the **Izod Center,** you can take in a variety of shows and even sporting events. Disney On Ice, Ringling Bros. and Barnum & Bailey Circus, and the Harlem Globetrotters have all performed there. Music lovers will appreciate the concerts, which have included Rascal Flatts and Miranda Lambert. The **Meadowlands Racetrack,** where people go to bet on the horses, isn't exactly family friendly. But your kids might catch a glimpse of the gallant beasts from the parking lot, and that is always a nice treat.

Costing $1.6 billion, the recently renovated Giants Stadium—now known as **MetLife Stadium**—is impressive. Seating 82,500, it boasts 5 premium lounges replete with brick pizza ovens, celebrity-chef cooking areas, and innovative technology—4 massive video display boards in each corner of the stadium, and more high definition (HD) per square footage than any other building in the US. Hosting more NFL games and having more visitors pass through its turnstile than any other stadium, it hosts major concerts, including Bon Jovi, international soccer, top-25 college football, and other events. You can also sign up to take a tour of the stadium. With a little planning, you can organize your trip around an event you'd like to see at the Meadowlands.

Medieval Times (ages 5 and up)
149 Polito Ave., Lyndhurst; (866) 543-9637; medievaltimes.com/lyndhurst.aspx. Open year-round, check the website for times and reservations. $$$$, children ages 3 and under free.

Help your kids travel back to a time when a knight in shining armor really did come along on his horse to sweep the fair princess off her feet. Be hosts of the king and his daughter and cheer as your team's knight takes part in an epic adventure that has him participating in a jousting contest. While you and your family indulge in a meal eaten entirely with your hands, you will learn about the costumes and culture of the medieval era. The flying falcon overhead and the galloping horses in the arena below are sure to captivate the hearts and minds of the audience. The best part? This is one dinner where your kids are encouraged to yell with wild abandon and no one will care one bit.

Shopaholic's **Paradise** ⬤

The state mascot might as well be the mall rat. After all, New Jersey has more malls per capita than any other US state. Because there's no state tax on clothing, people from other nearby states flock to the shopping centers for a bargain. New Jerseyans pride themselves on being able to spend entire days hanging out in the mall—from lounging in the food court to power shopping in the stores. If you'd like in on the action, here are some malls that might have you throwing down your credit card:

Bridgewater Commons Mall, 400 Commons Way, Bridgewater; (908) 218-0001; bridgewatercommons.com. If stores such as LEGO, Guess, and Michael Kors don't quench your shopping appetite, you can head to the village located adjacent to the mall, which is home to even more stores, including Crate & Barrel and Banana Republic. California Pizza Kitchen and McCormick & Schmick's Seafood Restaurant are among the eateries.

Cumberland Mall, Routes 47 and 55 (exit 27), Vineland; (856) 825-9507; cumberlandmallnj.com. Major department stores, such as JC Penney, and even a Home Depot call this mall home.

Jersey Gardens, NJ Turnpike exit 13A, 651 Kapkowski Rd., Elizabeth; (908) 354-5900; jerseygardens.com. This is the place to find a steal at outlet stores from Daffy's to Ann Taylor.

Jersey Shore Premium Outlets, 1 Premium Outlets Blvd., Tinton Falls; (732) 918-1700; premiumoutlets.com. You'll find 120 outlet stores, including Juicy Couture, Tommy Hilfiger, Calvin Klein, and Burberry.

Mall at Short Hills, 1200 Morris Tpke., Short Hills; (973) 376-7350; shopshorthills.com. A sophisticated and upscale mall, this one features Gucci, Chanel, and Tiffany & Co. among its tenants.

The Outlets at Bergen Town Center, Route 4 and Forest Avenue, Paramus; (201) 845-4051; bergentowncenter.com. Once considered the "dirt mall" of Paramus, the Outlets at Bergen Town Center has really turned around its reputation. Fresh and new, it features a Whole Foods and Target and outlet stores, including Nike, Carter's, and Gymboree. Don't miss the sweet-potato fries at Bobby's Burger Palace, which features a simple menu invented by celebrity chef Bobby Flay. The family might enjoy indulging its sweet tooth at Sugar and Plumm, a dessert shop and full-service restaurant.

Paramus Park Mall, 700 Paramus Park, Paramus; (201) 261-8000; paramuspark.com. A lively food court featuring Sbarro's and McDonald's and small kid's tables for easy family eating is a highlight of this mall, which includes Things Remembered and the Disney Store.

The Shops at Riverside Square, 390 Hackensack Ave., Hackensack; (201) 489-0151; simon.com. For the sophisticated shopper, the Shops at Riverside include Bloomingdale's, Saks Fifth Avenue, Hermes, Godiva Chocolatier, and Salvatore Ferragamo to name a few. The Fountain Spa, where you can indulge in a massage, and restaurants, including Maggiano's Little Italy, Morton's Steakhouse, the Cheesecake Factory, and Rosa Mexicano round out the mall's offerings.

Westfield Garden State Plaza, 1 Garden State Plaza, Paramus; (201) 843-2121; westfield.com/gardenstateplaza. This is one huge mall. In fact, you might be able to move into it. Here, you'll find a movie theater, restaurants, and stores, such as Macy's, Lord & Taylor, and Aeropostale.

New Bridge Landing (all ages)

Van Steuben House, River Edge; (201) 343-9492; bergencountyhistory.org. Call ahead for schedule of special events.

Three historic homes—the **Van Steuben House, Campbell-Christie House,** and **Demarest House**—are now all located near one another on this vast land. Visitors will notice that the sandstone architecture of all three homes is typical Dutch Colonial. And the New Bridge location was once a prosperous mill hamlet with a strategically placed bridge at the Hackensack River. This is the bridge that "saved a nation" because it served as a battleground, encampment ground, and military headquarters during the Revolutionary War. Even George Washington himself crossed the Hackensack River as the British invaded on November 20, 1776. Today visitors can learn both about the area's colonial roots and the importance of these three homes.

Van Saun County Park (all ages)

216 Forest Ave., Paramus, and Continental Avenue, River Edge; (201) 262-3771; co.bergen.nj.us/bcparks. Open Apr through Oct. $$, children under 3 and active military **free.**

With everything from pony rides to playground and picnic areas, Van Saun County Park offers a full day's worth of entertainment for families. After hosting a family reunion replete with burgers and dogs, you can head to the **Bergen County Zoological Park,** which is part of the Van Saun site. At the zoo, you'll feast your eyes on all sorts of animals, including a porcupine, eagles, monkeys, goats, and birds galore. Children will enjoy getting up close to the animals and partaking in some of the zoo's other attractions. Pony rides, a carousel, and a train round out the park's offerings. While those rides cost extra, they are well worth it for the smiles they put on the faces of the participating little ones.

Adults can have their fun, too, with areas for fishing and multi-use pathways that can even be used for bicycling. In addition, the family might enjoy the historic **Washington Spring Garden,** which is a zone that George Washington and his army passed through during the Revolutionary War. As a result of this final attraction, a trip to Van Saun can be both history and science lesson disguised as a day of entertainment, so the kids won't mind learning one bit.

Wortendyke Barn Museum
13 Pascack Rd., Park Ridge; (201) 930-0124. Free to view.
All that is left of the once 460-acre Wortendyke Farm, the barn is made of sandstone and was built around 1770 in typical Dutch style. Remarkably, the farm was owned by the Wortendykes for more than 115 years, from before the French and Indian War until before the Civil War. The barn, which is the hub of the museum, is made entirely of local wood, down to the nails. Once used to store crops, animals, and hay, the barn now includes handmade 18th- and 19th-century farm tools and exhibits showcasing the history of the Wortendyke Farm and Bergen County's farms.

Where to Eat

The Bicycle Club. 487 Sylvan Ave., Englewood Cliffs; (201) 894-0880; thebicycle club.com. Open Mon through Sat for lunch and dinner, and Sun for dinner only. Complimentary buffalo wings and carving stations make happy hour extra happy. $$

Dynasty Buffet. 383 Market St., Saddle Brook; (201) 226-1388. Open everyday for lunch and dinner. This all-you-can-eat buffet offers sushi, carving stations, and delicious already-prepared treats that include orange shrimp and crab wontons, alongside pigs in a blanket and sesame chicken. You can indulge in ice cream or pastries for dessert—and keep going back for more. $$

Meson Madrid. 343 Bergen Blvd., Palisades Park; (201) 947-1038; mesonmadrid .com. Open Sun through Thurs from 11 a.m. to 10:30 p.m., and Fri and Sat from 11 a.m. to 11:30 p.m. Here, you'll find delicious Spanish food, including paella and tapas in a charming setting. $$–$$$

P. F. Chang's. The Shops at Riverside, 390 Hackensack Ave., Suite 50, Hackensack; (201) 646-1565; pfchangs.com. Open Sun through Thurs 11 a.m. to 11 p.m., Fri and Sat from 11 a.m. to midnight. The deal for couples is perfect for parents, and kids will enjoy everything from the wonton soup to the mini desserts stuffed into shot glasses. $$

Villa Amalfi. 793 Palisade Ave., Cliffside Park; (201) 886-8626; villaamalfi.com. Open Tues through Sun for lunch and dinner. Among the best Italian restaurants in the area, Villa Amalfi offers bang for your buck. Don't miss the eggplant parmigiana or the fried calamari. $$

Where to Stay

Best Western Fort Lee. 2300 Rte. 4, Fort Lee; (201) 461-7000 or (888) HOTEL-NJ; bestwestern.com. This hotel is so close to the Meadowlands and Manhattan, including Broadway, that you'll never be at a loss for things to do. $$

DoubleTree by Hilton Hotel Mahwah. 180 Rte. 17 South, Mahwah; (201) 529-5880; doubletree.hilton.com. Close to many of the county's shopping centers and malls, this hotel attracts those who want to bargain hunt or pick up coveted items—from clothes to housewares. $

Hilton Woodcliff Lake. 200 Tice Blvd., Woodcliff Lake; (201) 391-3600; hiltonwood clifflake.com. A heated indoor pool, whirlpool, and racquetball courts are fun amenities at this hotel. $$$$

Teaneck Marriott at Glenpointe. 100 Frank W. Burr Blvd., Teaneck; (201) 836-0600 or (800) 992-7752; marriott.com. Spacious rooms, a spa, and fitness center make this a luxurious choice. $$$

Hudson County

With 12 municipalities, Hudson County is the smallest of New Jersey's counties. Still, more than 634,000 people call it home. And it packs, perhaps, the biggest punch when it comes to its attractions for families. While many associate the Statue of Liberty and Ellis Island with New York, those in the know have a secret; it is actually easier and more convenient to get to these icons of America from Hudson County's Jersey City. As if that was not enough, Hudson County's Hoboken prides itself on its famous people past and present, who include the likes of hometown boy Frank Sinatra and Bartolo "Buddy" Valastro, owner of Carlo's City Bake Shop and star of the TLC show *Cake Boss*.

The Statue of Liberty & Ellis Island (all ages) ⊘ ⊖ ⚠

Liberty State Park, Morris Pesin Drive, Jersey City; (201) 915-3440; libertystatepark .org. Statue is undergoing renovation, but you can still view it from afar. Park is open 6 a.m. to 10 p.m. daily. Prices vary based on activity; some are free. Immigrants have always been the backbone of America, and at one time, the Statue of Liberty welcomed them. "Give me your tired, your poor / Your huddled masses yearning to breathe free," goes the 1883 sonnet by Emma Lazarus, which is engraved on a plaque inside the Statue of Liberty. It is the spirit of America embodied in words, and it still gives you goose bumps. While immigrants no longer pass through Ellis Island, which is next door to the Statue of Liberty, the symbolism of these American landmarks is not lost on anyone. A trip to the tri-state area wouldn't be complete without a stop at the statue, a gift from France to the US more than 120 years ago in recognition of the friendship they developed during the American Revolution. Over the years, Lady Liberty began to signify freedom, democracy, and hope. Sharing this bit of American history with your children is a must, especially if you have family members who went through Ellis Island.

You can get to the Statue of Liberty and Ellis Island from Battery Park in New York City or from Liberty State Park in New Jersey. Many tourists don't know that, so it's usually easier to travel from the Jersey side. From here, you can park your vehicle and take a boat to the two islands—Liberty Island and Ellis Island. **Liberty State Park** has its own remarkable history that is linked to the statue and Ellis Island, which makes it the perfect pit stop on your journey.

Once a waterfront industrial area, Liberty State Park has been called the "lifeline of New York City and the harbor area" in the 19th and early 20th centuries, according to the Liberty State Park website. It was the home of the Central Railroad of New Jersey Terminal (CRRNJ), which brought many European immigrants who had been processed at Ellis Island to their new homes in the US. And you can still see the terminal at the park today. Although the area had been virtually abandoned when the railroad industry declined, the park was developed and opened to the public in 1976 in honor of the country's bicentennial.

At the Statue of Liberty, visitors usually can climb the lady and walk through the museum, where they will learn about the statue's history, from when France gifted it to the US to the present day. Although Liberty State Park and Ellis Island are opened, the inside of the statue is closed to the public for renovation until the end of 2012. Ellis Island offers visitors the chance to investigate their own families' immigrant roots by searching for names of relatives who may have passed through the island. You can also learn about the various countries from which these immigrants came, including their languages and customs. One of the most interesting aspects of the Ellis Island experience is a collection of the goods that immigrants brought with them, which includes everything from plates to clothing.

Liberty Science Center (all ages)

Liberty State Park, 222 Jersey City Blvd., Jersey City; (201) 200-1000; lsc.org. Open year-round, closed Mon. $15.75 for adults, $11.50 for kids ages 2 to 12.

Liberty Science Center is a nonprofit corporation that is designed to educate children about science. Aiming to get children excited about their studies, the Science Center, which is part of Liberty State Park, has you use only your sense of touch to get through a pitch-black maze, explore different kinds of energy, and act as a scientist with the chance to do everything from making a 6-foot soap bubble to creating your own artistic masterpiece. There's a play area for your youngest children—ages 2 to 5—where they can put together a car and test it, launch balls with an air cannon, and play a rock xylophone made of hanging stone slabs. Older kids will appreciate the IMAX and 3-D films that you can view for an additional price.

Hamilton Park (all ages)
Weehawken Township, Weehawken. Open year-round. Free to walk through.
Weehawken offers visitors the chance to be a part of history. Here, you can visit the site where Aaron Burr fatally wounded Alexander Hamilton at their notorious duel. The two met for an "interview," which was the euphemism for a duel, on July 11, 1804, in Weehawken, which was a popular site for other duels as well. In those times, according to historians, most duels never resulted in bloodshed. They were just a means to settle an argument. After years of political divisiveness between the two, Hamilton wrote some scathing words about Burr that he refused to take back, and Burr wanted to take it to the battlefield. When they

Hoboken:
The Birthplace of Baseball?

The first official baseball game was played at Hoboken's **Elysian Fields** on June 19, 1846. The game, which was played with Alexander Joy Cartwright's rules, had the Knickerbockers losing 23 to 1 against the New York Base Ball Club. Still, Cooperstown, NY, claims that's where baseball was born thanks to the rules being set there by Abner Doubleday. But on closer examination of the evidence, historians recognize Cartwright and that Hoboken game as the game's true beginning. Still, the two cities continue to vie for the right to baseball's birth. Today, although the Maxwell House Coffee Plant was built on what is believed to be the original spot of that first ball game, you can still visit the smaller Elysian Park at 10th Street and Hudson Street in Hoboken.

did, Burr won by fatally wounding Hamilton. Still, this was a final blow to Burr's already marred reputation and one from which he would never recover. Today you can visit the site of this historic duel, where you'll find a statue commemorating the duel and lots of open space for reflection.

Hoboken Historical Museum   (all ages)

1301 Hudson St., Hoboken; (201) 656-2240; hobokenmuseum.org. Open Tues through Thurs from 2 to 7 p.m., Fri from 1 to 5 p.m., and weekends from noon to 5 p.m. Admission costs $2 and is free for children.

Hoboken is rich with culture, and, for young adults just starting their career or family, it might be one of the trendiest places in the state to live. To get a glimpse at Hoboken's history, visitors can check out the Hoboken Historical Museum, which was founded in 1986 and features a rotation of exhibits designed to teach people about the city's traditions, culture, architecture, history, and historical landmarks. Past exhibits have included *A Sweet History of Hoboken,* a journey through the city's role as a candy manufacturer and home of entrepreneurs with successful bakery and sweets shops; *Hoboken in the 1970s;* and holiday crafts. With links to walking tours, including one of "Frank Sinatra's Hoboken," there's one-stop shopping for travelers. Kids might also enjoy story time at the museum.

Jersey City Museum   (all ages)

350 Montgomery St., Jersey City; (201) 413-0303; jerseycitymuseum.org. Open Wed through Sat from noon to 5 p.m. Admission costs $5 for adults, $3 for seniors ages 62 and up and students with a valid ID, and is free for children under 12.

At the Jersey City Museum, you can give your family a peek at local history through the prism of the visual arts. In addition to a collection of contemporary paintings and sculptures, the museum offers objects relevant to local history that come from places such as the American Pottery Company and the Jersey Glass Company. The collection proves a commitment to displaying the works of African-American, Asian, and Latino artists. The purpose of the collection, according to the museum's website, is to flaunt Jersey City's industrial roots, its ever-changing social landscape, and the influx of immigrants.

Landmark Loew's Jersey Theatre (all ages)

54 Journal Sq., Jersey City; (201) 798-6055; loewsjersey.org. Check website for shows, times, and prices.

Back in the day when Hollywood was glamorous and sophisticated, film studios built movie palaces, palatial theaters that featured orchestra pits, stages, and large screens. The exterior was often ornate. One of the last great movie palaces, the Landmark Loew's Jersey Theatre dates back to September 28, 1929, and originally cost $2 million to build. Known as the state's most lavish temple of entertainment, the theater had just under 3,100 seats, brass doors, and plush red carpeting. In 1993, after the theater was in decline and about to be closed, the city bought it for $325,000 after townspeople put up a big fight to keep the historic theater opened. The restored theater is now host to movies, performances for kids, musicals, and concerts. Check the schedule, find a show you and the family might like, and get a taste of old Hollywood glamour.

Lincoln Park (all ages)

Kennedy Boulevard and Belmont Avenue, Jersey City. Open year-round. Free.
Lincoln Park gets its name from the Lincoln Memorial, which stands at the main entrance, has Lincoln sitting on a pedestal, and was designed by James Earle Fraser. The park is divided into two parts, and its highlight is a promenade leading to a restored 1911 fountain (designed by sculptor Pierre J. Cheronin) featuring allegorical figures. Walking and running paths, picnic areas, zones for basketball and soccer, and tennis courts round out the park's offerings. At Lincoln Park West, you'll find a baseball complex, commercial driving range, batting cages, and a pond.

New York Waterway (all ages)

4800 Avenue at Port Imperial, Weehawken (there are also terminals in Edgewater, Lincoln Harbor [Weehawken], and Hoboken); (800) 533-3779; nywaterway.com. Open year-round. $$$$.
New York Waterway has terminals that transport travelers and commuters from various terminals in New Jersey to midtown and downtown Manhattan. What many don't realize is that the ferry also offers opportunities for sightseeing. Although pricey, the ferry offers views of the New York skyline and New Jersey suburbs, including the George Washington Bridge, that are spectacular and can make for a good photo opportunity, especially if the weather is good and you

sit on the top level of the ferry. You don't have to worry about the kids getting bored either. The ferry rides to midtown Manhattan take about 10 minutes.

In addition, New York Waterway provides transportation directly to the 9/11 Memorial in downtown Manhattan—and you can even get your **free** passes for admission through it. Prices vary, depending on from which terminal you leave. While the ferry ride might cost a little more, it's rather convenient, especially if you're traveling with kids and don't want to be bothered with the hassles of traffic or finding parking.

Park Performing Arts Center (all ages)

560 32nd St., Union City; (201) 865-6980; parkpac.org. Open year-round. Check website for shows, times, and prices.

Since 1932, the Park Performing Arts Center has brought theater to Hudson County and northern New Jersey. The center's very existence is thanks to **The Passion Play,** a theatrical performance about Christ's final days. Performed annually at the center and dating back to 1915 when German and Swiss immigrants decided to recreate the play that, since the 1600s, was performed in Oberammergau, Germany, *The Passion Play* has won over audiences. Over the years, it has evolved to eliminate anti-Semitic sentiment that was evident in the original and to be more inclusive of all people. In the 1990s, for instance, an African American played Christ. Staged by members of the local community, it has become a tradition for many in the area.

Although the center was originally dedicated to putting on *The Passion Play,* it now features all sorts of performances and even classes. The center's mission statement includes the goal of educating and entertaining everyone, especially children, about the theatrical arts. You can check the calendar to plan your visit, but you can find everything from comedians to dance troupes to singing groups putting on a show at any given time.

Where to Eat

Carlo's City Hall Bake Shop. 95 Washington St., Hoboken; (201) 659-3671; carlos bakery.com. Open Mon from 7 a.m. to 7:30 p.m.; Tues, Wed, Fri, and Sat from 7 a.m. to 9 p.m.; Thurs from 7 a.m. to noon; and Sun from 7 a.m. to 7 p.m. Home of Buddy "the Cake Boss" Valastro, the bakery serves up the best strawberry shortcake you have ever eaten, which makes the line circling the block worth it. $$

Chart House. Lincoln Harbor, Pier D-T, Weehawken; (201) 348-6628; chart-house
.com. Snapper, shrimp, and lobster are among the highlights on the menu, but you'll
be most struck by the amazing view of New York. $$$$

Houlihan's. 1200 Harbor Blvd., Weehawken; (201) 863-4000; houlihans.com; Open
Sun through Thurs from 11 a.m. to 2 a.m., and Fri and Sat from 11 a.m. to 3 a.m.
While this is one restaurant in the popular chain of Houlihan's restaurants, its location
is right on the water with an incredible view of Manhattan, and it provides outdoor
patio seating in the warmer months. $$

Robongi in Hoboken. 520 Washington St., Hoboken; (201) 222-8388, (201) 386-
8806, or (201) 386-8892; robongi.com/hoboken.aspx. Open Mon through Thurs 11
a.m. to 11 p.m., Fri from 11 a.m. to 11:30 p.m., Sat from 11:30 a.m. to 11:30 p.m., and
Sun from 11:30 a.m. to 11 p.m. You can indulge your cravings for sushi, while the kids
take on a bento box with veggies, rice, and chicken teriyaki. $$

Where to Stay

Courtyard Jersey City Newport. 540 Washington Blvd., Jersey City; (201) 626-
6600; marriott.com. This hotel is near the Statue of Liberty, New York City, and New
Jersey attractions to boot. $$$–$$$$

Hampton Inn Secaucus. 250 Harmon Meadow Blvd., Secaucus; (201) 867-4400;
hamptoninn1.hilton.com. Close to the Meadowlands—and the stadium—this hotel
also boasts putting guests in touch with nature at the nearby Meadowlands Environ-
mental Center. $$$

Sheraton Lincoln Harbor Hotel. 500 Harbor Blvd., Weehawken; (201) 617-5600;
starwoodhotels.com/sheraton. Within walking distance of the NY Waterway ferry, this
hotel is literally minutes from New York City. $$$

W Hoboken. 225 River St., Hoboken; (201)253-2400; whotels.com/hoboken. You will
get a beautiful view of the Manhattan skyline at this waterfront hotel, which would
be a major splurge for most families but speaks to the trendy and hip atmosphere of
Hoboken. $$$$

Essex County

With nearly 784,000 residents, Essex County is the second most populous in New Jersey. Most visitors who arrive in the state by plane meet Essex County first, as it is home to Newark Liberty International Airport. A county known for its diversity, Essex is home to cities as different as gritty Newark and typically suburban Livingston. There are the up-and-coming towns of Maplewood and Montclair, which is also home to Montclair State University. And Martha Stewart grew up in Essex County's Nutley. There are also a few fun things to do with the kids—from strolling a zoo to roller skating.

Branch Brook Park (all ages)

7th and Clifton Avenues, Newark; (973) 482-8900; usa-skating.com. Check website for hours and prices because they change often.

Roll back in time to when roller-skating was as cool as disco, pull on those skates, and bust a move with your kids. Whether you are a beginner or a pro, you are welcome to skate at Branch Brook Park. Call ahead to find out about the skating schedule, because the space is sometimes reserved for special events, such as Teen Night. Once you're there, you can take to the rink and skate freestyle, take skating lessons, celebrate your kid's birthday, play an arcade game, or have a bite at the pizza restaurant. Check the website for coupons.

Richard J. Codey Arena at South Mountain (all ages)

560 Northfield Ave., West Orange; (973) 731-3828; essex-countynj.org. Check website for hours. Call ahead about prices.

Opened year-round, the Codey Arena gives visitors the opportunity to ice-skate even at the height of summer. With 2,500 seats for spectators in one rink and 500 in another, the arena has been the official training site for the National Hockey League's New Jersey Devils since 1986. Recent renovations mean an improved entrance and the arrival of a concession stand, pro shop, and arcade.

Famous **New Jerseyans**

Long before *Real Housewives* and *Jersey Shore* castmembers arrived, New Jersey boasted many famous residents. And, by the way, most of New Jersey's popular people have a better rep than those reality stars do. Here are some familiar New Jerseyans:

Bruce Springsteen
Jon Bon Jovi
Queen Latifah
Frankie Valli
Mira Sorvino
Paul Sorvino
Michael Douglas
James Gandolfini
Bud Abbott and Lou Costello
Alan Alda
Tom Cruise
Zach Braff
Anne Hathaway
Nathan Lane
Bill Maher
Kelly Ripa
Paul Rudd
Susan Sarandon

Kevin Smith
Jon Stewart
Meryl Streep
John Travolta
Bruce Willis
Judy Blume
Fran Lebowitz
Gay Talese
Clint Black
Whitney Houston
Wyclef Jean
Jonas Brothers
Paul Simon
Frank Sinatra
Yogi Berra
Vince Lombardi
Phil Rizzuto

South Mountain Reservation (all ages)

S. Orange Avenue and Cherry Lane, West Orange; (973) 268-3500; essex-countynj .org. Open year-round. Free.

All the fun and charm of Essex County is packed into the more than 2,000 acres of South Mountain Reservation. Once home to the Lenape Indians, the area has retained most of its natural beauty—from the branch of the Rahway River that runs through it to the hardwood trees and tall hemlocks. Here, you'll find **Washington Rock,** which is a beacon built by George Washington to keep an eye on the British troops during the Revolutionary War and which was reactivated for the War of 1812. Other highlights of the reservation include the 25-foot waterfall at **Hemlock Falls** and the views of northern New Jersey, New York, and Staten Island that can be seen from the eastern ridge. But that's not all. Within the reservation, there are many attractions for families, including Turtle Back Zoo, Mini Golf Safari, and Codey Arena.

Turtle Back Zoo (all ages)

560 Northfield Ave., West Orange; (973) 731-5800; turtlebackzoo.org. Open daily from 10 a.m. to 3:30 p.m. Admission costs $8 for adults, $6 for children and seniors, and is free for children under 2.

Considered among the best zoos in New Jersey, Turtle Back Zoo has recently experienced a renaissance. Recent additions of an on-site animal hospital; complex with a gift shop, classrooms, auditorium, and reptile center; picnic areas; and an animal-themed playground make the zoo, which dates back to the 1960s, all the more enticing to families. The *Wild New Jersey* exhibit has guests observing native NJ species including bobcats, porcupines, and turkey vultures. At Essex Farm at the zoo, you can feed hand-raised farm animals, including goats and sheep. Kids can hop aboard a pony at the pony ride station next door. Children can also get a birds-eye view of the prairie dogs in the underground tunnels

leading to burrows next to their home. Opportunities for carousel and train rides, face painting, stretching pennies, and snapping pics in a photo booth are among the zoo's other treats for kids. Keep tabs on special events, such as the Holiday Lights Spectacular and the Pumpkin Patch, when kids get a **free** pumpkin upon admission.

Essex County Mini Golf Safari (all ages)
Cherry Lane and Northfield Avenue, West Orange; (862) 520-5024; turtle backzoo.org. Closed in the winter. Admission costs $7 for adults and $5 for children.

Part of the zoo and right next door, Essex County Mini Golf Safari is a 19-hole course that has players putting around giant African wildlife such as gorillas and hippos. Children can host their birthday parties at the minigolf facility, and there is food available for purchase for all visitors. Adults will appreciate the traditional public golf courses that are also nearby on the South Mountain Reservation.

Where to Eat

Il Vicolo Ristorante. 113 S. Livingston Ave., Livingston; (973) 740-0016. Open for lunch and dinner. Here, you will find traditional Italian dishes at affordable prices. $$

The Manor. 111 Prospect Ave., West Orange; (973) 731-2360; themanorrestaurant .com. Open for a la carte dinner, Wednesday lunch buffet, lobster buffet, Sunday brunch buffet, and a Sunday family dinner buffet. Check the website for times and prices of each and call for reservations. The Manor is elegant but also family friendly, and the food is divine. $$$–$$$$

Raymond's. 28 Church St., Montclair; (973) 744-9263; raymondsnj.com. Open for breakfast, lunch, and dinner Mon through Fri, and for brunch and dinner on Sat and Sun. Upscale diner food, a fresh-looking restaurant, and great prices are a winning combination with customers. $–$$

Regina Margherita. 246 Washington Ave., Nutley; (973) 662-0007. Call for hours. Many a diner has raved about how delicious the bread and pizza is at this eatery. $–$$

Where to Stay

Comfort Inn. 286 Rte. 46 East, Fairfield; (973) 227-4333; comfortinn.com. Bargain rates and comfortable accommodations make this a prime choice for families. $

Hyatt Regency Jersey City. 2 Exchange Place, Jersey City; (201) 469-1234; jersey city.hyatt.com. The indoor pool with views of the Manhattan skyline will blow your mind. $$$$

Residence Inn West Orange. 107 Prospect Ave., West Orange; (973) 669-4700; marriott.com. Old World, plantation-style design makes this hotel come alive. $$

Sheraton Newark Airport. 128 Frontage Rd., Newark; (973) 690-5500; starwood-hotels.com/sheraton. This hotel offers the convenience of being right at the airport and is perfect for families who will be taking connecting flights or will be in the area for a short time. $–$$

Morris County

K nown as the "military capital of the American Revolution" for its strategic location, Morris County has a rich and important history. Now the seventh largest county in New Jersey, it was considered a hot spot for the iron industry for years. Since mall rats hail from the Garden State, Morris County with its affiliation to retail——both shopping malls and outlet centers—is distinctly Jersey. It is also the home of many name-brand firms that have built their headquarters in the county. But Morris County is not all work and no pleasure. The more than 492,000 residents and their visitors have plenty to do in their free time—from exploring the past to visiting the children's museum.

Community Children's Museum (6 months and up)

77 E. Blackwell St., Dover; (973) 366-9060; communitychildrensmuseum.org. Open Thurs through Sat, 10 a.m. to 5 p.m. $5 for guests 6 months and up and $4 for seniors.

There is much for children to experience and enjoy at the Community Children's Museum. They can create static electricity, pretend they are orbiting the Earth in a replica of the Project Mercury spacecraft, sit on Van Gogh's bed, and put on a show on an actual theatrical stage. An art gallery featuring the works of other children rounds out the museum's offerings.

Glassworks Studio (ages 5 and up)

151 South St., Morristown; (973) 656-0800; umakeglass.com. Open Tues through Sun from Sept through May, with Wed evenings being reserved for adults only; open Mon through Sat from June through Aug, with Wed evenings being

reserved for adults only. Call ahead for holidays and hours. Price varies based on project.

For a change of pace, you and your family can stretch your creative muscles at Glassworks Studio, which allows visitors to make their own fused (kiln-formed) glass projects—from vases to plates. Although walk-ins are welcome, you should make a reservation, especially on weekends or holidays, to ensure you will be able to work your magic.

Great Swamp Outdoor Education Center (all ages)

247 Southern Blvd., Chatham Township; (973) 635-6629; morrisparks.net. Trails open year-round from sunrise to sunset; building is open year-round but is closed on weekends during the summer, otherwise open daily from 9 a.m. to 4:30 p.m. **Free** admission to walk on trails; cost of the educational programs varies.

More than 15,000 years old, the Great Swamp was born when the last glaciers melted into the basin of the Passaic Valley. Now, the Great Swamp is a mix of marshes, meadows, dry woods, and brush-covered swamp. This natural wonderland makes it a prime spot for a variety of plants and animals. As a result, it's a terrific place for a hands-on science lesson. You can opt for guided or self-guided hikes.

Historic Speedwell (all ages)

333 Speedwell Ave., Morristown; (973) 285-6550; speedwell.org. Open Tues through Sat from Apr to June, and Wed through Sun from July through Oct. Regular tour is $4 for adults, $3 for seniors (65 and over), and $2 for children (ages 4 to 16), children under 4 are **free;** special events sometimes have a higher price.

A visit to the site that once was the Speedwell Iron Works promises to be educational. For starters, you can see all that's left of the iron company—a few stone walls near Speedwell Lake. On the same grounds, however, you'll also find Judge Stephen Vail's farmhouse and **The Factory,** which holds at least one of the keys to the American Industrial Revolution. Teach your children about the invention of the telegraph at its birthplace, the Factory, the most important building on the property and the site where Alfred Vail and Samuel F. B. Morse perfected and showcased the electromagnetic telegraph in 1837 and 1838. Before this, the building was used by Alfred's father, Stephen, who added cotton looms and a gristmill to the space's garret and cellar. Interactive displays promise to take today's visitors on a journey from the beginning to the end of the telegraph's invention. A 24-foot waterwheel attached to the factory once powered the mill. Other historic homes—the Gabriel Ford Cottage, Moses Estey House, and L'Hommedieu-Gwinnup House—that were going to be torn down were moved to Historic Speedwell for preservation. There was a great effort on the part of the people of Morristown to keep this history alive, and visitors can take advantage of it.

Morris Museum (6 years and up)

6 Normandy Heights Rd., Morristown; (973) 971-3700; morrismuseum.org. Open Wed, Fri, and Sat from 11 a.m. to 5 p.m.; Thurs from 11 a.m. to 8 p.m.; and Sun from 1 to 5 p.m. Admission costs $10 for adults, $7 for children and seniors, and is free for children under 3.

Offering a little bit of everything—visual and performing arts, natural and physical sciences, and the humanities—Morris Museum is a nice place for families to entice their curiosity. Rotating exhibits have included 100 years of motorcycles, brain teasers, and 200 years of hats and purses. Among the 48,700 permanent exhibits are toys and dolls, a rock and mineral gallery, and costumes.

Morristown Green (all ages)

Morristown; (973) 539-2478; themorristowngreen.org. Open year-round. Walking through the Green is free.

At the center of Morristown lies Morristown Green, a historical landmark and the cultural hub of the town. Like much of the town, the Morristown Green had significance during the Revolutionary War. The Green was the home of Arnold's Tavern, which is where General George Washington stayed during his first encampment in 1777. Many military and political activities took place on the Green.

Morristown National Historical Park (all ages)

30 Washington Place, Morristown; (973) 539-2016; nps.gov/morr. Open year-round but call ahead about outdoor attractions during severe weather and the Wick House, which might be reserved. Washington's Headquarters Museum / Ford Mansion is free for children and $4 for adults ages 16 and up. Jockey Hollow is free to all.

The Morristown National Historical Park, the nation's first historical park, provides visitors with lessons in history and science. Famous for the role this area played in the American Revolution, the Morristown National Historical Park is first a prism on which you can learn about the birth of the US—and the sacrifices of the country's forefathers. It was here that Gen. George Washington and his troops endured the most difficult winter of the war. The wooded area also provides a firsthand look at nature. Broken up into 4 units—the Ford Mansion and Museum, Jockey Hollow, the New Jersey Brigade/Cross Estate Gardens, and Fort Nonsense—the area allows you to easily plan your trip according to what you want to see most.

Washington lived in the **Ford Mansion** during the Jockey Hollow winter encampment of 1779–1780. The Georgian-style mansion, which was built by the prominent Ford family in the early 1770s, was largely made of wood and only recently did park officials install a sprinkler system to guard against fire. With high beams and wide wooden-plank floors, the home exudes colonial, almost as much as the thought that Washington and his confidantes, such as Alexander Hamilton, walked the floors while birthing the nation. Although the mansion has been a museum for more than 140 years, it was where Washington faced, perhaps, his greatest challenges—the worst winter in recorded history, near-mutinous soldiers who were starving and sick, and a British invasion.

Jockey Hollow is home to most of the hiking trails—20 miles of trails to be exact—in Morristown National Historical Park. During the winter of 1779–1780, this area was home to 10,000 Continental Army soldiers. You can also take in views of wildlife and go hiking in this zone of the park. At the same time, you can get an idea of what colonial life was like at the soldier's huts.

When Washington was breaking up the camp in May, he had the troops build a fort in case of an attack on Morristown. That attack never happened, and a legend grew that Washington only had the soldiers build the fort to keep them busy. From this tall tale came the name "Fort Nonsense." Today you can visit **Fort Nonsense** and see what's left of one of Washington's forts.

At the New Jersey Brigade unit of the park, you will find the glorious and unexpected **Cross Estate Gardens.** Visually appealing, the Cross Estate is an integration of native and formal gardens. Highlights include a wisteria-covered pergola and a mountain laurel allée. You can sign up for garden tours and special events.

Whippany Railway Museum (all ages)
1 Railroad Plaza, Whippany; (973) 887-8177; whippanyrailwaymuseum.net. Open
year-round. Admission is $1 for adults and 50 cents for children under 12.

As home of the Morris County Central, a steam tourist railroad, Whippany is a
natural fit for this museum. Although the museum was relocated to Newfound-
land, NJ, for a time, it returned to its current home in 1985. Various railroad
equipment and cars are on exhibit on the actual railroads. Inside, the museum
showcases memorabilia from a different local railroad each year. The Whippany
passenger station and the water tank that once helped power steam locomotives serve as notable landmarks. During the year, the museum hosts various
events, such as the Santa Claus Special, which has families riding a train with
Santa himself, and a pumpkin festival featuring train rides and a crafts fair.

Where to Eat

Black Horse Tavern & Pub. 1 W. Main St., Mendham; (973) 543-7300; blackhorsenj
.com. Tavern is open for dinner only Tues through Sat, pub is open for lunch and dinner every day. In business for more than 260 years, this tavern offers sophisticated
meals and should be offered to children and adults with a discriminating palette,
whereas the pub is more casual. $$–$$$$

George & Martha's American Grille. 67 Morris St., Morristown; (973) 267-4700;
georgeandmarthas.com. Open every day. This restaurant puts a fresh spin on Ameri-
can classics. $$–$$$

Grain House at the Olde Mill Inn. 225 Rte. 202, Basking Ridge; (908) 221-1150;
oldemillinn.com. Open Mon through Fri for lunch and dinner; on Sat for a la carte
breakfast, lunch, and dinner; and on Sun for brunch and dinner. Offering American
fare in an authentic 18th-century setting, Grain House delights with its kid's menu,
which features shrunken hot dogs, grilled pizza, and even tenderloin medallions. $$$

Where to Stay

Best Western PLUS Morristown. 270 South St., Morristown; (973) 540-1700;
hotelmorristown.com. With only 60 guest rooms, this is a cozier hotel option located
in the center of historic Morristown. $$

Courtyard by Marriott. 3769 US 46 East, Parsippany; (973) 394-0303; marriott .com. The kids will enjoy the indoor pool and whirlpool even if you head to this 146-room hotel in the cooler months. $

Embassy Suites. 909 Parsippany Blvd., Parsippany; (973) 334-1440; embassysuites1 .hilton.com. The **free** made-to-order breakfast, which includes an omelet station, and **free** Manager's Reception in the evening for guests make meal times afford-able and easy. $$$

Hyatt House Morristown. 194 Park Ave., Morristown; (973) 971-0008; hyatt.com. Suites with kitchens, a fitness center, and breakfast bar make this a family friendly option. $$

Westin Governor Morris. 2 Whippany Rd., Morristown; (973) 539-7300; westin governormorris.com. A sophisticated hotel, the Westin is close to attractions and shopping, including the Mall at Short Hills. $$$$

Warren County

ormed in 1825, the small county of Warren has more than 108,000 residents. Home to part of the Delaware Water Gap, Warren County's wide-open spaces and natural beauty are its draw. In fact, the county ranks 9th in area—at nearly 365 square miles—but 19th in population. Although the various seasons have their charms in Warren County, its fall foliage might make autumn the best time of year for a visit. The jewel tones of the leaves make for one spectacular rainbow and a great photo op for families.

Allamuchy State Park (all ages)

Willow Grove Street, Hackettstown; (908) 852-3790; nj.gov/dep/parksandforests. Open daily sunrise to sunset. Admission is free for all, even on Canal Days and Canal Heritage Days.

Anyone who enjoys fishing—and prefers to catch trout—will enjoy a stay at Allamuchy State Park, home of the Musconetcong River. Considered some of the best trout fishing in the state, the river provides year-round catches for fishermen. Warm water species, such as largemouth bass, sunfish, perch, and pickerel live in Cranberry Lake, Jefferson Lake, Allamuchy Pond, and Deer Pond. Opportunities for hiking, boating, canoeing, deer and small-game hunting, and even rock climbing also abound. Like most of the state parks, you can also pack lunch and picnic amid nature.

On Canal Days in June, or on Canal Heritage Days, which take place eight times in the summer and fall, you can learn how the Lenape, also known as the Delaware Indians, lived 400 years ago. And you can see how they transitioned their home into a bustling port city with the arrival of the Morris Canal. The

Waterloo Village area, where this happens, features 19 historic buildings, including a blacksmith's shop, a meeting house, and even a concert venue.

Delaware River Railroad Excursion (all ages)

675 Corliss Ave., Phillipsburg; (877) TRAIN-RIDE or (908) 454-4433; 877trainride .com. Regular season is May through Oct, but the Polar Express rides take place in late Nov and Dec. Corn Maze, Great Pumpkin Ride, and Mine Train tickets cost $20 for adults and $13 for a child; Polar Express tickets cost $25 for adults and $19 for children; children under 2 can ride on your lap for $1, but if you plan to bring a baby in a car seat, which will take up its own train seat, then you are expected to purchase a ticket.

This excursion gives travelers a chance to ride New Jersey's only operating steam locomotive. The passenger cars are Long Island Railroad commuter coaches from the 1950s that have been restored. While the ride itself can be fun, there are many special events that take place on board throughout the year, including the Polar Express, the Great Pumpkin Train, and a day with Thomas the Tank Engine.

Jenny Jump State Forest (all ages)

State Park Road, Hope; (908) 459-4366; state.nj.us/dep/parksandforests. Open daily from 8 a.m. to 4:30 p.m. Camping fees only; shelters for $40 per night, family camp sites are $20.

Those courageous enough to hike the narrow trails to the top of Jenny Jump Mountain meet great rewards. They will witness nature at its finest with views of the Highlands, Kittatinny Mountains and Valley, the Delaware Water Gap, and the Great Meadows. If that's too much of a hike for your family, don't despair. You can simply stay lower to the ground. What's unique about the forest is the fact that it was formed of glaciers 21,000 years ago. Today you can see the evidence of the thick ice that once filled the area and carved out valleys and rocks from mountain tops when it melted, bringing on a dramatic and surprising terrain. The melting glacier birthed the Great Meadows, which is quite fertile and was cleared in the 1800s for cultivation of vegetables, and the Pequest River. The forest is also home to rocks that are estimated to be 1.6 billion years old, some of the oldest rocks on Earth. Families who love the outdoors might enjoy camping in the forest and can consider the campsites or shelters available. Hiking, bicycling, fishing, boating, and canoeing are possibilities for visitors. Hunters find turkey, deer, and small game in the forest. Packing a picnic for snacking in the

Happy **Highlands**

Stretching from Phillipsburg in Warren County in the southwest to Mahwah in Bergen County in the northeast, the **Highlands Region** covers 88 municipalities and seven counties—Bergen, Hunterdon, Morris, Passaic, Somerset, Sussex, and Warren. It is responsible for providing more than half of the state with drinking water. Ripe for exploring, the region is a showcase for a variety of geographic and geologic details, such as rolling hills, pastoral valleys, ridges, diverse forests, and wildlife habitats. There are state parks and remnants of history (both from the Native Americans and Revolutionary War heroes) in the region. And you can do everything from hop on a hot-air balloon ride to cut down your own Christmas tree in the Highlands. For more information on Highlands tourism, visit highlands tourism.org.

quiet, shaded area of the park is a lovely way to spend the day with your loved ones. Just remember, the forest is home to many black bears, so keep your eyes peeled and be safe.

At the **Greenwood Observatory,** which was the baby of the United Astronomy Clubs of New Jersey and stands at 1,100 feet, visitors can use a telescope to check out the stars. It is one of the few spots in New Jersey where there is no light source pollution, which means clear skies.

Lakota Wolf Preserve (all ages)

8 Mount Pleasant Rd., Columbia; (877) 733-9653; lakotawolf.com. Open year-round but call ahead for schedule. Admission for the Wolf Watch only costs $16.05 (tax included) per adult (ages 12 and up), and $7.49 (tax included) per child ages 2 to 11; admission for the Wolf Watch and a day at Camp Taylor (swimming the lake, bringing picnic lunch, hiking trails, mini golf, etc.) costs an additional $6.65 per adult and $1.36 per child.

Dream of being part of the pack? Visitors to the Lakota Wolf Preserve find themselves in an observation area that is in the middle of packs of wolves. You can observe tundra, timber, and arctic wolves in their natural habitat. And the guides will teach you about their habits and home. You might also see bobcats and foxes, which also live at the preserve. As a winner of the New Jersey Governor's Environmental Tourism Award, you are certain to have an unforgettable and educational experience with the wolves.

Land of Make Believe & Pirate's Cove (ages 2 and up)

354 Great Meadows Rd., Route 611, Hope; (908) 459-9000; lomb.com. Open weekends only from Memorial Day weekend through the second weekend in June; open daily from the third Sat in June through Labor Day. Free parking; admission costs $22.50 for adults, $20.50 for seniors (ages 62 and up), and $24.50 for children (ages 2 to 18) and includes all rides, shows, attractions, family picnic grove, and admission to Pirate's Cove.

The Land of Make Believe and Pirate's Cove is 30 acres of water attractions and family-oriented entertainment. Getting wet under the emptying 1,000-gallon water bucket at Blackbeard's Pirate Fort or a thrilling tube experience on Blackbeard's Action River Ride are refreshing on a hot summer's day. Little ones will enjoy their own space in the wading pools and slides made just for them. Adventurers will appreciate riding a tug boat through the perfect storm or taking the plunge on a winding body slide. The truly brave can check out the Pirate's Peak, downhill water slides that are 40 feet high and more than 400-feet long. Of course, the pièce de résistance of the park is the Black Hole, which was rated the best waterslide in the country, according to the park's website, and is reserved for those who are 8 years old and up. For more laid-back entertainment, families can try their hand at the arcade or hop on a kiddie ride, such as the Jump Around Frog.

Victorian Days at Belvidere (all ages)

Warren County Courthouse, Belvidere; (908) 475-4124; victorianbelvidere.com. Takes place annually in Sept. Prices vary, depending on the activities in which you participate.

The community of Belvidere, NJ, invites visitors to step back in time to the Victorian period with its ornate homes, proper manners, and distinctive garb. At the Vintage Baseball Game, spectators take in the national pastime as it was played in the 19th century. The players follow the rules, wear the uniforms, and use the equipment of that

era. A fashion show puts on display everything from the ornate hats to wedding dresses of the Victorian period. The porches of the Victorian homes in the area serve as the perfect backdrop for Victorian tea parties to which all are invited. And those who are into hot wheels will enjoy the vintage car show. On the house tours, you're likely to see Victorian houses that look like something you'd mirror in gingerbread, along with a Swedish log cabin and an original Sears Roebuck catalog kit house. If you're not easily spooked, you can also sign up for the cemetery tour, which is run by the "Undertaker," to learn about the town's historic final resting grounds. It's not all macabre. Some of the stories told on the tour will bring on a chuckle.

Where to Eat

Mama's & Cafe Baci. 260 Mountain Ave., Hackettstown; (908) 852-2820; mamas cafebaci.com. Open Sun through Thurs from 11 a.m. to 11:30 p.m., and Fri and Sat from 11 a.m. to 12:30 a.m. The menu is Italian-centric but offers some surprises, such as jalapeño poppers, and the prices are more than reasonable. $$

Mattar's Bistro Lounge. 115 Rte. 517, Allamuchy; (908) 852-2300. Open for lunch and dinner Mon through Sat from 11:30 a.m. to 11 p.m. and Sun from 11:30 a.m. to 9 p.m. Typical children's fare, including mac and cheese, make this a great place for families, regardless of how picky the eaters. $$

Where to Stay

Comfort Inn Hackettstown. 1925 Rte. 57 West, Hackettstown; (908) 813-8500; comfortinnhtown.com. Deluxe continental breakfast and **free** in-room fridge, microwave, and coffeemaker are benefits of this hotel. $–$$

Hotel Belvidere. 430 Front St., Belvidere; (908) 475-2006; hotelbelvidere.com. Family owned and operated, the Hotel Belvidere was established in 1831 and provides guests with the comforts of home. $–$$

Hunterdon County

Hunterdon County is not as well known as some of the other New Jersey counties. But it has some interesting distinctions that make it worthy of attention. For starters, the Lindbergh kidnapping trial took place in Hunterdon County's Flemington Courthouse. Then known as the "trial of the century," it centered on the kidnapping and murder of the son of aviator Charles Lindbergh. In the end, Bruno R. Hauptman was executed for the awful crime that is still talked about today. Another reason Hunterdon County is noteworthy is for its role in the center of it all: It is about a one-hour commute each from Hunterdon County to Philadelphia and to New York City. With a population of nearly 128,350 people, Hunterdon County is small but big on history.

Flemington Courthouse (all ages)

Main Street, Flemington; co.hunterdon.nj.us/facts/chpics.htm. Open year-round. Free admission for all.

Although the town no longer puts on reenacts of the trial of the century—it did until recently—you can still get a feel for what went on when the world had its eyes on Flemington Courthouse; this was the O. J. Simpson trial of its day. It was here that Bruno R. Hauptmann was tried and found guilty of the kidnapping and murder of aviator Charles Lindbergh's son. The restored courthouse features the witness chairs, press area, and even the cell where Hauptmann spent his days. Across the street, you can see the **Union Hotel,** where participants in the case—press, attorneys, and members of the public—stayed during the trial.

Hunterdon Arts Museum (all ages)

7 Lower Center St., Clinton; (908) 735-8415; hunterdonartmuseum.org. Gallery open Tues through Sun from 11 a.m. to 5 p.m. Suggested admission is $5 per person.

In this historic 19th-century mill, you can view contemporary art and design. The contrast of the old mill with modern art is a lovely touch that won't be lost on your family. The permanent collection features mostly prints (by Mark di Suvero, Philip Guston, Alex Katz, Ad Reinhardt, and others) but also includes paintings and drawings. With a great mix of emerging and established artists, the rotating exhibits are thought provoking, too. The museum also offers art classes.

Marshall House Museum (all ages)

60 Bridge St., Lambertville; (609) 397-0770; lambertvillehistoricalsociety.org. Open on weekends Apr through Oct from 1 to 4 p.m., and by appointment throughout the year; on the first Sun each month from Apr to Oct (or by appointment), you can take a guided walking tour of the town. Admission is free for the museum and $5 per person for the walking tour.

Today the Marshall House is home of the Lambertville Historical Society, but it was the childhood home of James Wilson Marshall, who discovered gold in California in 1848. Built in 1816, the house is architecturally interesting, with a pegged front door and chimney cupboards in the parlor. In 1882, St. John's Roman Catholic Church bought the property for a convent, and it served this purpose until 1964, when the church gave the home to the New Jersey Department of Conservation and Economic Development for preservation. Now, you can visit and take a tour of the historic home. You can sign up through the historical society for walking tours that include other homes and sites of historical significance.

Northlandz (all ages)

495 US 202, Flemington; (908) 782-4022; northlandz.com. Closed Tues, open weekdays from 10:30 a.m. to 4 p.m., and Sat and Sun from 10:30 a.m. to 5:30 p.m. Admission costs $13.75 for adults (ages 13 and up), $12.50 for seniors (ages 62 and up), $9.75 for children (ages 2 to 12), free for children under age 2.

At what is advertised as the "World's Largest Model Railroad," up to 100 trains travel more than 8 miles of track. Created by Bruce Williams Zaccagnino, who dreamed of making a track like this while fiddling with his own model trains when his home was being built, the trains are only one part of the museum. There is also a doll museum, a pipe organ, and art galleries.

Roxey Ballet (all ages)

243 N. Union St., Lambertville; (609) 397-7616; roxeyballet.org. Check website for shows and ticket prices, which vary.

Originally known as the Hunterdon Youth Ballet when it launched in 1995, the company has evolved into a touring professional dance troupe with a roster of well-known artists. The group even performed for President Barack Obama's inauguration in 2009. Hunterdon County was blessed with ballet thanks to Mark and Melissa Roxey, who had performed with companies such as Joffrey Ballet, American Repertory Ballet, and Dayton Ballet. Family-friendly performances have included *Cinderella* and *The Nutcracker*.

Samuel Fleming House (all ages)

5 Bonnell St., Flemington; (908) 782-4049; flemingcastle.com. Call ahead for tour schedule. Tours are free, but donations are welcome.

Until recently the Samuel Fleming House was known as Fleming Castle. Samuel Fleming built the house around 1756, but it was a house and never a castle, although, according to most accounts, it was structurally superior to other homes of the time. And you can bet it was probably like a castle to the Fleming family. Nowadays the house is an educational center for children. Group tours are available by appointment. Activities at the house have included a teddy bear picnic; a visit with Martha Washington, who shares her husband's story; and displays of children's artwork.

Where to Eat

Hamilton's Grill Room. 8 Coryell St., Lambertville; (609) 397-4343; hamiltonsgrill room.com. Open Mon through Thurs from 6 to 9 p.m., Fri and Sat from 5 to 10 p.m., and Sun from 5 to 9 p.m. Any place that serves fried green tomatoes and butternut squash gratin is worth checking out. $$$

Historic Perryville Inn. 167 Perryville Rd., Perryville; (908) 730-9500; theperryville inn.com. Closed Monday; open for lunch Tues through Fri from 11:30 a.m. to 2:30 p.m. and for dinner Tues through Thurs from 5 to 9 p.m., Fri and Sat from 5 to 10 p.m., and Sun from 4 to 8 p.m. With menus for both sophisticated diners and those with a more casual meal in mind, the historic inn, which dates back to 1813, delivers something for everyone. $$–$$$

La Casa Bianca. 144 Main St., Whitehouse Station; (908) 534-8384; lacasabianca.net. Closed Mon; open Tues through Fri for lunch from 11:30 a.m. to 3 p.m., and for dinner Tues through Thurs from 5 to 10 p.m., Fri and Sat from 5 to 11 p.m., and Sun from 4 to 10 p.m. The highlight of this menu is the brick-oven Tuscan-style pizza. $$–$$$

Milford Oyster House. 92 Rte. 519 (Water Street), Milford; (908) 995-9411; milford oysterhouse.com. Open Sun through Thurs from 5 to 9 p.m., and Fri and Sat from 5 to 10 p.m. If steamed clams, broiled Alaskan cod, and spinach salad sound delish, then you will probably enjoy a meal at this restaurant. $$$

Where to Stay

Courtyard Lebanon. 300 Corporate Dr., Lebanon; (908) 236-8500; marriott.com. With a state-of-the-art lobby and affordable prices, families are drawn to this hotel. $$

The Lambertville Waterfront. 11 Bridge St., Lambertville; (609) 397-4400; lambert villestation.com. Lovely accommodations right on the water make this small hotel worth considering. $$–$$$

Somerset County

A mecca for history buffs, Somerset is one of New Jersey's oldest counties. The charter, in fact, dates back to May 22, 1688. But it's more than a remnant of colonial times. With 11,600 acres of parkland, much of which features golf courses, trails for hiking and bicycling, areas for picnics, stables, and an Environmental Education Center, it offers fun for those who seek fresh air and time amid nature. Every year, the County Fairgrounds hosts the Somerset County 4-H Fair, which has been a tradition since 1948 and today features dog, horse, and livestock shows, and entertainment, such as twirling, go-karts, rockets, magic, and line dancing. If farming and nature are among your interests, you can join the more than 323,444 people who call Somerset County home.

Boudinot Southard Ross Estate (all ages)
135 N. Maple Ave., Basking Ridge; (908) 221-1770; historicalsocietyofsomersethills .org. Call ahead for events and schedule.
Built in 1777 by Elias Boudinot, the Boudinot Southard Ross Estate attracted Martha Washington, who reportedly visited the home many times while George Washington's army was stationed in Morristown. Whether this is true or not makes little difference. The home is still historically significant. After Boudinot, other owners included Samuel Lewis Southard, who served as a US senator, state attorney, and governor; John C. Spooner, a former US senator from Wisconsin; and William D. Bancker, who founded the Pennbrook Golf Club (in Basking Ridge). The Ross family owned the home until 2005 when they sold the house to the county for more than $6 million.

Duke Farms (all ages)

80 Rte. 206 South, Hillsborough; (908) 722-3700; dukefarms.org. Call ahead to register for programs because public access is by reservation only. Ticket prices and reservation details vary by program.

James Buchanan Duke built Duke Farms in 1893 and spent the rest of his life transforming the place into a work of art. He excavated nine lakes, and he built 45 buildings, stone walls, and more than 18 miles of roadway. The area also features sculptures and fountains. When he died in 1925, his daughter Doris inherited the farm and, as an adult, opened display gardens she created in her father's greenhouses to the public. She also purchased other farms on the borders of the estate and expanded. When she passed away in 1993, she asked that Duke Farms become a haven for native flora and fauna, according to the farm's website. There are educational programs, such as the Turkey Trot, which has visitors checking out the natural habitat of wild turkeys, and orchid classes, for enthusiasts of that flower. Hiking trails and bike tours are other fun ways to explore the wildlife and plants at the farm.

Jacobus Vanderveer House & Museum (all ages)

955 US 202/206, Bedminster; (908) 212-7000, ext. 404. Open year-round but call ahead for schedule of events. Admission costs $10 for adults, $8 for seniors, and is free for children under 12.

Situated in River Road Park, the Jacobus Vanderveer House is typical of the Dutch farm houses that covered the NJ countryside before the Revolutionary War. Much of the original house remains, but the oldest part dates back to the 1770s. There are important architectural details worth noting, including the wide pine flooring, raised wood paneling above the fireplace, and a barrel-back cabinet. Additions made to the house in later years tell the story of the era in which they were built, which makes the tour all the more interesting. Jacobus Vanderveer was the son of Cornelius Vanderveer of Long Island. Jacobus and his wife moved to what is now New Jersey, and, as a landowner, he became a leader in the community. The whole Vanderveer family holds a special place in the Revolutionary War effort because of their staunch support of breaking away from the British.

Indeed, during the war, Gen. Henry Knox, a bookseller turned revolutionary, rented the Vanderveer house. He was in the area as ordered by George Washington, who asked Knox to establish a Continental artillery. Essentially, Knox created what is considered the first training camp for military in the country. In fact, he went on to become the first commander of West Point. While visiting the historic Jacobus Vanderveer House, you can stop by the **Pluckemin Artillery Cantonment,** site of the precursor to West Point. The camp featured barracks, an armorer's shop, military forge, and lab. Most of the remnants of the Revolutionary War are long gone, but locals are hoping to use the area again to educate people about history and the significance of the land.

Kennedy Martin Stelle Farmstead (all ages)

450 King George Rd., Basking Ridge; (347) 927-8748; kmsfarmstead.wordpress.com. **Check website or call ahead for events and their prices, which vary by event.**
An example of English and modified Dutch framing, the Kennedy Martine Stelle Farmstead is a farm house, wagon, house, and barn. The farmstead has connections to prominent people from the past, namely Rev. Samuel Kennedy, a local minister and educator, and Revolutionary War hero and politician Col. Ephraim Martin. The barn hosts events, such as art exhibits, theatrical and musical performances, lectures, and even dancing.

Somerville Fire Department Museum (all ages)

N. Doughty Avenue, Somerville; (908) 526-7098 or (908) 526-4828 after 5 p.m. **Open Sat from 10 a.m. to noon or by appointment.**
Visiting the inside of this old firehouse is like walking into a history book. Suddenly, you can have a look at the meeting space, signage, and equipment of yesteryear. A model fire engine gives you the idea of what previous versions of the heroes' trucks looked like. And an actual-size, old-fashioned fire engine (that looks more like a wagon) will mesmerize you. You won't believe how they put out fires with this kind of resource.

US Golf Association Museum (all ages)

77 Liberty Corner Rd., Bernards Township; (908) 234-2300; usgamuseum.com. **Open Tues through Sun from 10 a.m. to 5 p.m., closed Mon. Admission costs $7 for adults, $5 for USGA members, $3.50 for children ages 13 to 17, and free for children ages 12 and under.**
Golf enthusiasts will enjoy this museum, which aims to educate the public about the history of golf in the US and especially about the victors of the US Golf Association (USGA) championship. Permanent exhibits include galleries that highlight the careers of Arnold Palmer, Bob Jones, and Ben Hogan. Bob Jones's putter,

"Calamity Jane II," and artifacts from today's golfers, including Tiger Woods, are among the other highlights. A museum dedicated to golf would be incomplete without a putting green. In fact, outside the museum lies a 16,000-square-foot Pynes Putting Course. You can try your hand on the green and even putt with replica antique clubs and balls.

Washington Rock State Park (all ages)

355 Milltown, Rd., Bridgewater; (908) 722-1200; state.nj.us/dep/parksandforests. Open daily sunrise to sunset. Admission is free for all.
With a 30-mile panoramic view of Raritan Valley, Washington Rock State Park is a draw just for its location. But it also carries some historical heft. George Washington used this site as a lookout in the winter of 1777 when the British army was moving toward Westfield. Purchased in 1913, Washington Rock State Park is one of the oldest state parks in New Jersey. It's considered a great place to kick back and relax, have a picnic, and enjoy the view.

Where to Eat

De Island Breeze. 676 Franklin Blvd., Somerset; (732) 214-8611; deislandbreeze .com. Open every day for lunch, which is served until 3 p.m., and dinner. For something different, head to this restaurant, which serves Caribbean cuisine and sometimes has live musical entertainment on hand. $$

Sophie's Bistro. 700 Hamilton St., Somerset; (732) 545-7778; sophiesbistro.net. Open Tues through Fri for lunch (from 11:30 a.m. to 3 p.m.) and dinner, and on Sun for brunch from 11:30 a.m. to 2:45 p.m. Offering a taste of France, Sophie's Bistro features escargot and pizza de Provence on its menu. Don't worry, there are burgers and fries, bearing funny French names, for the kids. $$$

Where to Stay

Bridgewater Marriott. 700 Commons Way, Bridgewater; (908) 927-9300 or (888) 887-7869; marriott.com. Meat-and-potatoes kinds of families will appreciate the dishes at T'bones Steaks, and the indoor pool is a bonus. $$

Days Inn Hillsborough. 118 US 206 South, Hillsborough; (908) 685-9000 or (800) 329-7466; daysinn.com. This hotel boasts simple accommodations at an unbeatable price. $

Hampton Inn Somerset. 255 Davidson Ave., Somerset; (732) 563-1600; hampton inn.hilton.com. Clean and comfortable, the Hampton Inn promises to help maximize sightseeing in the area. $$

Hyatt Summerfield Suites Bridgewater. 530 Rte. 22 East, Bridgewater; (908) 725-0800; bridgewater.summerfieldsuites.hyatt.com. A 24-hour convenience store and a **free** hot breakfast top the amenities at this hotel. $$$

Union County

A rivalry between Elizabethtown and Newark is at the heart of Union County's birth. The story goes way back to 1664 when the Lenni Lenape Indians gave English settlers title to the land that extended from the Raritan to the Passaic Rivers and westward. The county's site points out that the Indians did not understand the concept of "owning" land and that they were selling the rights to use the land for hunting, fishing, farming, and other activities. It would become the first permanent settlement of the English in New Jersey, and Elizabethtown became an economic powerhouse and the first seat of the state's government. Still, what is known today as Union County began as part of Essex County. When the town of Plainfield was created in 1847, people started calling for a separation into more than one county. The tension mounted when Newark replaced Elizabethtown as Essex County's seat. In the end Union County was born of these animosities. The enduring history is evident in many of the county's major attractions.

Bowcraft (all ages)

2545 Rte. 22 West, Scotch Plains; (908) 389-1234; bowcraft.com. Closed in the winter. Free admission and parking; pay for ride tickets either on an individual basis (20 tickets for $19, 40 tickets for $35, 100 tickets for $75) or with a fun-pass for unlimited riding ($22.95 for a day-pass, opening to 4 p.m., $22.95 for a nite-pass, 3 p.m. to close).

An amusement park, Bowcraft features a variety of kiddie rides, including a merry-go-round, kiddie boats, and a big trucks ride. The family might also enjoy bumper cars, tilt-a-whirl, and a train to name a few other attractions. Arcade and street-fair games are great when you have had your fill of rides. The food available on-site includes pizza, chicken wraps, and salads.

Cedar Brook Park (all ages)

Pemberton Avenue, Plainfield; ucnj.org/community. Open year-round. Free to walk through the park.

Apparently to celebrate the 300th anniversary of Shakespeare's death in the early 1900s, gardens dedicated to him were established across the US. Few still remain, but the Plainfield Garden Club continues to maintain the **Shakespeare Garden** at Cedar Brook Park. Originally, only old varieties of plants from England were used. Stakes with Shakespearian quotes stood near plants. The garden has continued to grow and evolve over the years. There's much for the eye to take in.

Kidzvillage (all ages)

131 S. 31st St., Kenilworth, and 507 King Georges Rd., Woodbridge; (908) 445-7220 and (732) 826-8577; kidzvillage.com. Open Sun through Thurs from 10 a.m. to 7 p.m., Fri from 10 a.m. to 9 p.m., and Sat from 9 a.m. to 9 p.m. Adults must be accompanied by a child, and admission is free for them; admission costs $9.99 for children ages 2 and up and $6.99 for walkers under 2, free for infants.

An indoor playground that is designed to look like a city specifically for kiddies—replete with supermarket and salon—Kidzvillage offers children the chance for creative play. In the Kidz Kastle, you can go to battle with others and launch spongy balls as if they were cannons. The entire place is filled with activities to trigger the imagination and encourage make believe. Other attractions include a diner where kids can serve pretend meals, a comic store where they can dress up as superheroes, and a salon where they can become hairdressers for lifelike mannequins. Parents will be as entranced as the kids.

Liberty Hall Museum at Kean University (ages 6 and up)

1003 Morris Ave., Union Township; (908) 527-0400; kean.edu/libertyhall/home.asp. Open Mon through Sat from 10 a.m. to 4 p.m. Admission costs $10 for adults, $6 for seniors, $6 for children (ages 3 to 17).

Home to New Jersey's first elected governor, William Livingston (who incidentally also signed the US Constitution), Liberty Hall is filled with antiques, ceramics, textiles, toys, and tools owned by generations of Livingston and Kean families (Livingston's niece who married a Kean later had her son buy the home for her). Built in 1772, Liberty Hall was originally 14 rooms in the Georgian style. Over the

The First **New Jerseyans**

The Lenni Lenape, whose name means "true people," were the first settlers in the state. These Native Americans lived in tribes and were a peaceful people. Also known as Delaware Indians for their homes along the Delaware River, the Lenni Lenape also called parts of New York, Pennsylvania, and Delaware home. Believed to have been the original Algonquin tribe, the Lenni Lenape were revered among their people and probably lived in New Jersey and parts of these other states for thousands of years before the Europeans arrived. In fact, other Algonquin tribes refer to the Lenni Lenape as "grandfathers," which made them effective in settling rivalries and disputes.

Making their homes near streams and bodies of water, the Lenni Lenape lived in wigwams, long homes made of bark. They either lived as a single family or among several related families. Hunters, gatherers, fishermen, and gardeners, the Lenni Lenape provided for their families. They prided themselves on tending to the children, with whom they played games to teach life lessons. Games similar to pick-up-sticks, dice, and lacrosse were common, according to a site designed by Terrie Wilson for the Reading Area Community College.

Eventually, the British would drive the Lenni Lenape out of their homeland. But first they would struggle with the arrival of the Swedes, the Dutch, and the English Quakers. On more than a few occasions, the Lenni Lenape trusted their neighbors, only to later discover they were being tricked out of land. Today, there are still about 16,000 Lenni Lenape in New Jersey, Pennsylvania, and Oklahoma, where the government previously relocated them. The ones in New Jersey and Pennsylvania are not officially recognized by the government, which means they have no reservation land or governmental system of their own. But they still carry on their traditions and culture. Indeed, you will find remnants of the Lenni Lenape and the mark they made on the state all over New Jersey. Throughout this book, you will read about the Lenni Lenape and places you can visit to learn more about them.

years, it grew to 50 rooms and became a Victorian mansion. A Lenox tea set dating back to the Depression (and created as a charity to aid out-of-work architects and draftsmen), a doll house that is a replica of a New York brownstone, and a Federal-style pier table are highlights of the hall's collections. You can even have your wedding or party on the grounds. On Wednesday, you can join other guests at an afternoon tea overlooking the elaborate gardens.

Miller-Cory House　(ages 7 and up)　
614 Mountain Ave., Westfield; westfieldnj.com. Open seasonally. A nominal admission fee is charged.

The Millers and the Corys were among the earliest settlers in Union County. The house is named after these two families because they were both its owners at different times in the 18th century. Both were rural farmers, but they were well known in the community. Today it is a nationally recognized museum. Every Sunday, costumed docents tell visitors about life in the 18th and 19th centuries. Trained artisans demonstrate the crafts and skills of a typical farm family of those eras. The cooks at the Miller-Cory House have received lots of media attention over the years for their open-hearth cooking.

Reeves-Reed Arboretum　(all ages)　
165 Hobart Ave., Summit; (908) 389-1234; reeves-reedarboretum.org. Open daily from dawn to dusk. Admission is free, with a suggested donation of $5.

The Reeves-Reed Arboretum dates back to 1889, when John Hornor Wisner built his residence on the site. He hired Calvert Vaux, a partner in the firm that planned Central Park, to landscape the area. Wisnor's wife planted the first daffodils, which are a popular springtime attraction at the arboretum. This is a reflection of the following owners desire to continue to grow the daffodil collection. It wasn't until 1974 that the Reed family, the last owners of the property, and other locals raised money to purchase it as an arboretum. Now, you can visit the gardens with your family and do so much more. There are all sorts of activities, including a teddy bear tea, Daffodil Day, and a fall campout for families.

Warinanco Park　(all ages)　🚲🐟🌿🎣👥
3rd Avenue at Park Street, Roselle; ucnj.org. Open year-round. Free to walk through the park.

Designed by Frederick Olmstead, one of the landscape architects who designed Central Park, Warinanco Park offers a bit of everything all year long. There are winding trails; fields for playing football, soccer, and baseball; tennis courts; and gardens. In winter, you can take a spin on the ice-skating rink. But the park truly shines in the spring. Every April, the park's **Henry S. Chatfield Memorial Garden** is awe-inspiring as more than 14,000 tulips from Holland bloom. A little later, a rainbow of azaleas bloom from April through June.

Where to Eat

La Griglia Seafood Grill and Wine Bar. 740 Boulevard, Kenilworth; (908) 241-0031; lagriglia.com. Open for lunch Mon through Fri from 11:30 a.m. to 3 p.m., and for dinner Mon through Thurs from 5 to 10 p.m., and Fri and Sat from 5 to 11 p.m. Open Sun for private parties. This restaurant offers a variety of dishes starring the freshest seafood. $$$

Marco Polo. 527 Morris Ave., Summit; (908) 277-4492; marcopolonj.com. Open for lunch and dinner. Continental cuisine with an Italian flair in a family-friendly restaurant is what keeps the customers happy. $$

Mario's Tutto Bene. 495 Chestnut St., Union; (908) 687-3250; mariostuttobene .com. Open daily for lunch and dinner. An eclectic menu that features Italian-centric dishes and even tapas gets customers talking and eating. $$$

Where to Stay

Best Western Riverview Inn & Suites. 1747 Paterson St., Rahway; (732) 381-7650 or (800) 722-1889; bestwestern.com. **Free** complimentary breakfast, a fitness center, and a pool are among the conveniences offered by this hotel. $$

Hampton Inn Linden. 501 W. Edgar Rd., Linden; (908) 862-3222; hamptoninn1.hilton .com. "On the run" breakfast bags are a nice touch for families on the go. $$

Kenilworth Inn. Garden State Parkway exit 138, Boulevard and S. 31st Street, Kenilworth; (800) 775-3645; kenilworthinn.com. An outdoor swimming pool and continental breakfast buffet top the amenities here. $

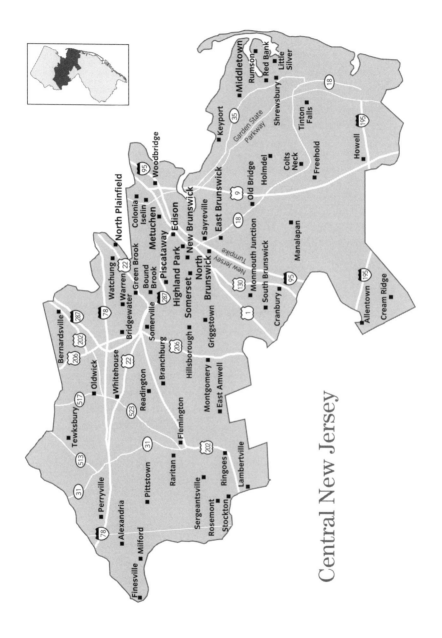

Central New Jersey

Central
New Jersey

Mercer County

Home to the state capital Trenton, Mercer County is called the "Capital County." It is also famous for being the county in which Gen. George Washington and members of the Continental Army crossed the Delaware River and marched to Trenton to defeat the Hessians. This surprise attack led to the so-called 10 Crucial Days, a period of time that included the battles at Trenton and Princeton and revived the Continental Army, making ultimate victory possible. Today, Mercer County is home both to historical sites commemorating these pivotal points in the country's birth and the state's governor. Physically located in the center of the state, Mercer County and its more than 366,500 residents can also boast being at the center of the state's history. And you can be, too, when you visit.

Brearley House (ages 6 and up)

100 Meadow Rd., Lawrenceville; (609) 895-1728; thelhs.org. Open year-round.
Built in 1761 by John Brearley, New Jersey's first chief justice and an original signer of the US Constitution, the Brearley House remained in his family for 150 years. Today you and your family are welcome visitors to the Brearley House, its surrounding meadow, and the not-too-distant Delaware and Raritan (D&R) Canal site. Outside there is a wide variety of trees that serve as a great opportunity for a science lesson. The brickwork and banister in the basement are original to the house; the bricks used to build the house were made of clay from the grounds on the property. One of the nicest traditions at the Brearley House is the New Year's Eve celebration, in which visitors gather around a Hogmanay Bonfire to bid farewell to the last year. It is a Scottish tradition; the word *hogmanay* means "last day of the year" in Scottish.

Drumthwacket (ages 6 and up)

354 Stockton St., Princeton; (609) 683-0057; drumthwacket.org. Open Wed for guided tours, individuals and groups of 15 begin their tour at noon, but reservations are required, so call ahead. Admission is free with a suggested $5 donation.

Built on land near the location of the Battle of Princeton, Drumthwacket is the New Jersey governor's residence. The property was owned originally by William Penn, founder of Pennsylvania, but it was acquired by William Olden. In 1835, Charles Smith Olden began the construction of Drumthwacket, which gets its name from Scottish Gaelic words that mean "wooded hill," according to the Drumthwacket website. In 1860 Olden became the state's governor, and as a result, was the first governor to live in Drumthwacket. What is most interesting is how long it took for it to become the official governor's residence. It wasn't until 1966 that the last owner sold it to the state of New Jersey, but the state didn't raise enough funds for it to become the governor's residence until 1981. The Drumthwacket Foundation has completely restored the house and gardens and furnished it with period antiques. Today, more than 10,000 people visit the historic estate for tours every year.

As part of the Drumthwacket estate, visitors will see the **Olden House,** a small white farmhouse across the front lawn of Drumthwacket. Originally built by John Hill sometime between 1759 and 1765, the home was purchased by Thomas Olden, a tailor, farmer, and son of one of the original settlers who established the Quaker community of Stony Brook. Charles Smith is one of Thomas's grandsons. Over the years, Olden House was used as a butler's residence and a home for rare birds and later monkeys. When it was opened to the public in those days, the children referred to it as the "Monkey House." The 1996 restoration of Olden House is considered a model for others. Every detail was tended to; the colonial kitchen and mantel were taken apart and put back together exactly as they were, and original paint colors were researched and matched. Being at Drumthwacket makes you feel as if you're a genuine revolutionary.

Howell Living History Farm (all ages)

70 Wooden's Ln., Lambertville; (609) 737-3299; howellfarm.com. Open year-round but closed sporadically during the year, so call ahead. Prices vary by program.

The Howell Living History Farm gives families the chance to witness life on a farm in the 1800s. You can explore the vast property, which features 19th-century hog houses, working oxen in a refurbished barn, sugar maple trees that actually produce syrup, the blacksmith workshop, corn crib, wagon house, and sheep barn. You can even see how hay would have been thrown and stacked in the barn during hay season. Maybe you'll even be able to imagine yourselves taking to the farm life.

Kuser Farm Mansion (ages 6 and up)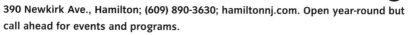

390 Newkirk Ave., Hamilton; (609) 890-3630; hamiltonnj.com. Open year-round but call ahead for events and programs.

Rudolph Kuser immigrated to the US from Zurich, Switzerland, in the 1800s. He and his family maintained a farm on what is now Kuser Road in Hamilton. Across the way, Kuser's son built what is today the Kuser Farm Mansion as a vacation home. The Kusers were very influential and played a part in New Jersey politics and business. Today, visitors can experience a bit of what life was like for the Kuser family by taking a tour of the mansion. If you've dreamed of having a home theater, you will appreciate the one the Kuser family had back in the day—an 18-foot curved CinemaScope screen, which puts an image twice the usual width onto a 35 mm frame. Other highlights include the chicken house, gazebo, tennis court, and laundry house. If your kids like trains, they'll enjoy the basement and its display of the Jersey Valley Model Railroad. But call ahead to be sure the basement is opened, because it's often closed for special events.

Lee Turkey Farm (all ages)

201 Hickory Corner Rd., East Windsor; (609) 737-3299; leeturkeyfarm.com. Walking and harvest tours from July through Oct; hayride tours from Sept through Oct, strawberry tours the second and third week of June. Tour prices range from $5 to $9, depending on which you choose.

The Lee family has been running this farm since 1868, and the farm itself dates back to 1802. With all its original barns still in use, Lee Turkey Farm bills itself as a fine-quality supplier of home-grown vegetables, fruits, and oven-ready turkeys. Shoppers pick their own fruits and vegetables from the land. Or, if they're in a rush, they can stop in the on-site market. The farm raises about 5,000 turkeys annually, and they are available for purchase all year long. Seasonal tours give kids the chance to see different aspects of the farm. A walking tour or hayride tour give visitors an overview of the farm, but there are also more specialized tours, such as the Strawberry Tour, which educates guests about spring fruits and vegetables, honeybees, and baby turkeys. On the Harvest Tour, you actually get to pick your own fruits and vegetables and opt into pumpkin picking if you'd like. The only catch here is that you must leave Fido at home; pets are not allowed on the farm.

Mercer County Equestrian Center (all ages)

431 Federal City Rd., Pennington; (609) 730-9059; nj.gov/counties/mercer/commissions/park/equestrian.html. Open Mon through Fri from 7 a.m. to 8 p.m., and Sat and Sun from 7 a.m. to 5 p.m. Prices vary based on activity; 10-minute pony rides cost $10.

For a chance to take in a horse show or let the kids take a ride on a pony, you can head to the Mercer County Equestrian Center. There are 27 horses on-site. And you can take a self-guided tour of the grounds. This is also home to the **Mercer County Educational Gardens.**

Mercer County Park Marina & Boathouse (all ages)

Lake Mercer; (609) 989-6559; nj.gov/counties/mercer/commissions/park/boat_marina.html. Open weekends and holidays from the end of May through mid-June noon to 6 p.m.; open from mid-June through Labor Day Wed through Fri from noon to 5 p.m., and Sat and Sun from noon to 6 p.m. Closed Mon and Tues. Prices vary based on activities and rentals.

On Lake Mercer, you can visit the boathouse or launch small boats on the **free** ramp. The man-made lake is also a great place to take advantage of the available kayaks, row boats, and pedal boats. You might even catch the Olympic rowing team training at the Finn Casperson Rowing Center. When you get off the water, you can indulge in a picnic, bike on the trails, hop on the playground, or play some volleyball.

Morven Museum & Garden (ages 6 and up)

55 Stockton St., Princeton; (609) 683-4495; historicmorven.org. Open Wed through Fri from 11 a.m. to 3 p.m., and Sat and Sun from noon to 4 p.m. Admission costs $6 for adults, $5 for seniors (ages 60 and up) and students. No strollers in the museum.

Until 1982, when Drumthwacket (p. 71) opened, Morven was the state's governor's mansion. William Penn sold the property to Richard Stockton, whose family resided there for four generations. Stockton's grandson and namesake, who signed the Declaration of Independence, was among the residents. Besides the governors, the only nonfamily member to live at Morven was Gen. Robert

Wood Johnson, the chairman of Johnson & Johnson. The estate was named by the second Richard Stockton's wife, Annis Boudinot Stockton, a prolific poet who chose "Morven" after a mythical Gaelic kingdom in the poems of Ossian, a legendary poet of Ireland. Guided tours of the historic residence are available all year except during the Festival of Trees during the holiday season, when visitors can walk through the rooms on their own to view the holiday trees that are decorated by local businesses and garden clubs. Keep tabs on the website for special exhibits, which have included displays on loan from other museums and a showcase of 100 versions of the American flag.

National Guard Militia Museum of New Jersey (all ages)
National Guard Training Center, Sea Girt Avenue and Camp Drive, Sea Girt; (732) 974-5966; nj.gov/military/museum. Open 7 days a week from 10 a.m. to 3 p.m. Closed on state holidays. Admission is free for all.
The National Guard Militia Museum of New Jersey aims to preserve the history of the Army National Guard, Air National Guard, and Naval Militia of the state and to educate the public about how the military and wars shape the community. With the largest collection of New Jersey–related Civil War research material in the country, the museum's highlights, not surprisingly, include a Civil War cannon and submarine. In addition, you will view replica and original military uniforms, artifacts, and equipment. Outside, you will find tanks and other vehicles. You might also want to visit the nearby **Lawrenceville Annex,** which is home to weapons, uniforms, and equipment pertinent to various eras in military history, and the **War Memorial Annex,** where visitors can take in exhibits featuring portraits and artifacts related to important figures in the state's military history.

Princeton Battlefield State Park (all ages)
500 Mercer Rd., Princeton; (609) 921-0074; nj.gov/dep/parksandforests. Open daily sunrise to sunset. Admission is free for all.
Commemorating the January 3, 1777, surprise attack on the British, which had Gen. George Washington and his soldiers tasting victory and culminating what came to be known as the 10 Crucial Days, Princeton Battlefield State Park is fraught with historical significance. This site of the Battle of Princeton extends to what is now Princeton University.

As a park, this landmark provides the usual outdoor fun—trails for hiking, birding, open lawns, and space for cross-country skiing. But it is also a window on the birth of the US. Visitors can stop by the **Thomas Clarke House,** which was built by Quaker Thomas Clarke and was the site where Hugh Mercer, friend to Washington and a Continental Army soldier, was treated for wounds he suffered during the Battle of Princeton, which eventually killed him. At the house, you will see exhibits related to the Revolutionary War and period furniture. At the center of the battlefield stood a Mercer Oak that you can still see today. **The Ionic Colonnade,** designed by Thomas U. Walter, who also designed the Capitol building, is also on-site, as is a patio marking the fallen British and American soldiers buried there. The **Princeton Battle Monument,** which is an impressive statue featuring Washington as he leads his troops into battle and the death of Gen. Hugh Mercer.

Princeton Doll & Toy Museum (all ages)

8 Somerset St., Hopewell; (609) 333-8600; princetondollandtoy.org. Open Mon, Fri, and Sat from 10 a.m. to 5 p.m. Museum admission costs $5 for adults and $3 for children, who must be accompanied by an adult. Membership costs $25 and entitles members of the immediate family to admission for a year.

Play is the work of children, and the Princeton Doll & Toy Museum reveres that labor. Here you and your family can see the evolution of dolls and toys from the 1600s to the present. You can check out everything from antique wooden dolls to toys related to storybooks at the museum. One of the most popular exhibits is the Alice in Wonderland House, where you can share tea with Alice and the White Rabbit. Collectors might enjoy the dolls and accessories available at the gift shop or the library, which houses more than 400 volumes on toys and dolls and is **free** to use. You can even have a toy or doll repaired or appraised at the museum.

State House Tours (ages 6 and up)

125 W. State St., Trenton; (609) 847-3905; njleg.state.nj.us/legislativepub/visiting statehouse.asp. Hourly tours available Mon through Fri from 10 a.m. to 3 p.m., and first and third Sat of each month from noon to 3 p.m.; closed Sun and state holidays. Admission is free, but reservations are required and should be made far in advance of your visit.

Remarkably, the New Jersey State House cost the equivalent of about $400 when Jonathan Doane built it in 1792. Over the years, the State House faced many changes; at one point, there was even a fire that destroyed part of the building. In the 1960s, a plan was put forth to demolish the entire building and start over; that plan was never executed. Now that people are more interested in preserving historic buildings, parts of its original form still stand. In the 1980s, the building was renovated to modernize its structure, mechanics, and electrical wiring. Tours that educate visitors about the art, architecture, and history of New Jersey's State House and the legislative process are available to the public. You'll need to make reservations, and the tours get booked quickly in the spring, so call well in advance of your planned trip. Ahead of your tour, your children might enjoy the "Kids' Page" on the State House's website, which teaches lessons in an entertaining way about the legislature and how a bill becomes a law.

Terhune Orchards (all ages)

330 Cold Soil Rd., Princeton; (609) 924-2310; terhuneorchards.com. The farm store and yard are open every day year-round, but activities, such as apple picking, happen seasonally. Prices vary.

Terhune Orchards offers the best of both worlds: You can pick your own produce fresh off the tree or vine or you can pick up the fresh stuff at the farm store. The pick-your-own options include strawberries in May, cherries and blueberries in June, raspberries and blackberries in July, apples in September, and pumpkins in October. You can also pick flowers. The store is a great option, too, because it is located in a barn that is more than 100 years old and sells everything, from lots of homemade goodies, including apple cider, salsa, and pies, to plants and flowers for your own garden.

If the produce doesn't draw you in, there are lots of activities that will help you and your children become one with nature. You can visit barnyard animals, such as donkeys and sheep, ride a tractor, and participate in special seasonal activities, such as a corn stalk maze and theme story barn in the fall. The farm walking trail promises visitors the unforgettable experience of observing nature firsthand. There is a variety of plants and trees along the way and a meadow of wildflowers that sends a lovely scent your way. If you plan your trip according to the "Diggers and Planters" schedule, your child could get a glimpse of life as a farmer with hands-on lessons in gardening. The "Read and Pick" program has children listening to stories about the fruit or vegetable that they will later be picking. You can even celebrate your birthday with a party on the farm, which includes a wagon ride and special snacks.

Trenton Thunder Minor League Baseball (ages 4 and up)
1 Thunder Rd., Trenton; (609) 394-3300; milb.com. Season is Apr through Sept; check website for schedule. Tickets cost $12 for club seats, $11 for adult pavilion seats, and $10 for junior/senior pavilion seats; tickets each cost $1 extra if you purchase them on game day.

The Trenton Thunder is the Class AA affiliate of the New York Yankees, which means it provides fans of the national pastime high-quality baseball. In fact, according to the team's website, the Thunder has been recognized as the "Nation's Best Franchise." Every once in a while a genuine Yankee in need of rehab might take to the field in Trenton. On the banks of the Delaware River, you can sing, "Take Me Out to the Ball Game" while catching one. Children ages 7 to 12 can also sign up for 2-day baseball camps in the summer. As part of the camp, participants get a ticket to a Thunder game, where they are also recognized on the field. And their family and friends can get a special rate for their admission. Even if baseball isn't your thing, you might enjoy the fare at Waterfront Stadium. You can savor everything from traditional french fries and hot dogs to crab fries and hand-dipped ice cream. Being so close to Pennsylvania, this stadium also offers Philadelphia water ice, a dessert made with finely crushed ice and sweeteners, such as sugar or fruits. And the Strike Zone Snack Express provides items, such as hot dogs and grilled cheese, portioned and priced especially for kids. A picnic area is a nice addition. But, of course, baseball is the ticket here. This is your chance to say you saw baseball's rising stars before they became big leaguers. Sports heroes like Nomar Garciaparra and even Derek Jeter got their start with the Thunder.

William Trent House Museum (ages 6 and up)
15 Market St., Trenton; (609) 989-3027; williamtrenthouse.org. Open daily from 12:30 to 4 p.m.; closed on holidays. Admission costs $4 for adults, $3 for seniors, and $2 for children.

Not much is known about William Trent except that he was a wealthy merchant and slave owner. He married twice, and his second wife, who was just 19 when they married, was alleged to have had relations with the rector of Christ Church, who was sent back to England in disgrace. There is also controversy surrounding Trent's death. Some believe he had a stroke, while others think African slaves might have poisoned him. In any event, his country estate in New Jersey is now a museum that you can visit. Built in 1719, the William Trent House was the residence of many different people, including the first provincial governor of New Jersey under England's monarchy, Lewis Morris, who used it as his official residence even though, ironically, the governor of Pennsylvania owned the property then. During the American Revolution, the William Trent House was first occupied by Hessian soldiers, only to later be turned into a supply depot for Washington and the Continental Army. Other New Jersey governors resided there after the war. And the last private owner, Edward A. Stokes, donated the residence to the city of Trenton to be used as a museum. Using the inventory of the estate when Trent died and facts about his contemporaries' homes in the area, curators have furnished the home with items that are true to the period when it was first built. You can also tour the garden, which has an 18th-century design and is used to teach visitors about the era's gardening methods and plants that were used both for food and medicine. There are also special events throughout the year, including an annual open house, when the residence is decorated for the holidays.

Where to Eat

Chambers Walk Cafe. 2667 Main St., Lawrenceville; (609) 896-5995; chamberswalk .com/home.html. Open for lunch Mon through Fri from 11:30 a.m. to 2:30 p.m. and dinner Tues through Sat from 6 to 9 p.m. The Bistro Basics menu, which is available Tues through Fri, offers tasty fare at reasonable prices. $$–$$$

Elements. 163 Bayard Ln., Princeton; (609) 924-0078; elementsprinceton.com. Open for lunch and dinner, except on Sat, when it is open only for dinner. "Hip" is the word that comes to mind when you see this restaurant and its menu. $$$

Fedora Cafe. 2633 Main St., Lawrenceville; (609) 895-0844; fedoracafe.webs.com. Closed Mon; open Tues through Thurs from 8 a.m. to 10 p.m., Fri and Sat from 8 a.m. to 11 p.m., and Sun from 8 a.m. to 1 p.m. (for brunch only). Highlights include Sunday brunch featuring french toast stuffed with peaches and topped with cinnamon butter, maple syrup, and crème fraîche, and panini with ingredients such as chicken, portobello mushrooms, onions, and cheese. $$

Mediterra. 29 Hulfish St., Princeton; (609) 252-9680; mediterrarestaurant.com. Open for lunch Mon through Sat from 11:30 a.m. to 4 p.m., and Sun from noon to 4 p.m. Open for dinner Mon through Thurs from 5 to 10 p.m., Fri and Sat from 5 to 11 p.m., and Sun from 4 to 9 p.m. This upscale restaurant offers Mediterranean cuisine, and you can eat your meal outside overlooking Princeton's Palmer Square in the warmer months. $$$

Where to Stay

Comfort Inn. 3270 US 1 North, Lawrenceville; (609) 896-3700; comfortinn.com. **Free** breakfast with hot waffles and an exercise room in which you can work them off are pluses here. $$$–$$$$

Red Roof Inn Princeton. 3203 Brunswick Pike, Lawrenceville; (609) 896-3388; redroof.com. Pets stay **free,** and parking is also **free** at this hotel. $$

Trenton Marriott Downtown. 1 W. Lafayette St., Trenton; (609) 421-4000; marriott .com. The benefit of this hotel is its vicinity to attractions, such as the State House in New Jersey and Sesame Place in Pennsylvania. $$

Middlesex County

S mack in the center of New Jersey, Middlesex County demands to be the center of attention. It is also the midway point between Boston and Washington, DC, and Philadelphia and New York. Location isn't all it boasts. Middlesex County is home to Rutgers University, where you can cheer on the up-and-coming Scarlet Knights in basketball, soccer, or football, and historical sites, such as Edison Memorial State Park. The Raritan River runs the entire length of the county, and it has played a major role in its development. As population grows—Middlesex County is one of the fastest growing of New Jersey's counties with more than 809,850 people as of the 2010 US Census—so has the parks system. There are 18 county parks that encompass 6,600 acres of land. Beyond the green, open spaces, there is a lot to do and see in Middlesex County.

Cornelius Low House (ages 6 and up)

1225 River Rd., Piscataway; (732) 745-4177; co.middlesex.nj.us/culturalheritage. Open Tues through Fri and Sun from 1 to 4 p.m.; closed Mon, Sat, and state holidays. Admission is free for all.

Raritan Landing was a booming port city in the late 1700s and early 1800s, and Cornelius Low was a wealthy merchant of Dutch ancestry and a prominent citizen. His home, which was built in Raritan Landing in 1741, is now the Middlesex County Museum. The 2-story stone house built in the Georgian style is a showplace for rotating exhibits. One example is *Film in New Jersey: 1890 to 1960*, which documents Fort Lee and other New Jersey cities as the first Hollywood, land of the motion picture. While the architecture and history of the house itself is of value, visitors can also anticipate special programs, including workshops and events, such as folk arts performances.

Edison Memorial State Park (all ages)

Thomas Edison Center, 37 Christie St., Menlo Park, Edison; (732) 494-4194; menlo parkmuseum.org. Open Thurs through Sat from 10 a.m. to 4 p.m. The museum is undergoing renovation, so call ahead. Free admission, with a suggested donation of $5.

Thomas Edison, who patented about 400 inventions, including the phonograph, made Menlo Park, NJ, his home in 1876 when he was still virtually a nobody. In his time in Jersey, he became known as the Wizard of Menlo Park and set the course for making Middlesex County forever famous. He perfected the lightbulb and invented the motion picture camera. When he died in 1931, he held 1,093 patents.

Edison Memorial State Park is most noteworthy for its **Memorial Tower** and museum, both honoring Edison and his work. Edison quit working at Menlo Park after deciding that he and his inventions needed to be closer to New York City, the center of business. He eventually would relocate to West Orange, NJ. Much of the invention factory at Menlo Park would be abandoned and nearly forgotten. But first Edison's friend Henry Ford would take two of the buildings and artifacts and move them to Michigan. It wasn't until recently that Menlo Park would truly get a makeover.

The site became a tourist attraction even while Edison was still headquartered there. Once his inventions started to shape modernization and word spread of his commitment to science, people made the trek to see what was happening there. In 1925, the state of New Jersey honored Edison and his family with a tablet and memorial for the work he did at Menlo Park. You can still see the tablet at the corner of Christie Street and Route 27, which is also known as Lincoln Highway. In 1938, the Memorial Tower, dedicated to Edison, was topped with a replica of a lightbulb. In the 1950s, Raritan Township, the town where Menlo Park stood, became Edison Township to further honor the inventor who captured the world's attention.

Today the Tower, which began crumbling a while back and has been closed to the public for years, is being restored to its former glory. In addition, a new museum will open its doors. The first thing visitors will see when they enter the museum is the Memorial Tower, which will be visible through large glass windows. The space will pay homage to Edison and his inventions but will also offer guests the chance to use their own creativity and problem-solving skills to try their hand at invention. There will be interactive exhibits and explanations about how Edison's work is relevant to today's technology.

Besides the Tower, tablet, and museum, there are 36 acres of parkland, which have gone virtually unnoticed until now. The plan is to construct an outlook beside the meadow and expand the trails. The area around the Tower, which is full of memorabilia from Edison's day, will be prominently on display. In that area, there will be open-air exhibits that will have visitors learning about the physics of sound and light through whisper dishes and echo tubes, for example.

Roosevelt Park (all ages)

Route 1, Edison Township; co.middlesex.nj.us/parksrecreation. Open year-round. Free to walk through the park.

Roosevelt Park is unique for its offerings. It has the usual park attractions—tennis courts, basketball courts, playing fields, picnic areas, playgrounds, trails for bicycling and walking, and a lake for fishing. But it also boasts a Veterans Memorial, an ice-skating and roller-skating rink (which are specifically located at 151

Run **Free!**

Wide-open spaces are a hallmark of Middlesex County. If you'd like to take advantage of the fresh air and nature the area has to offer, here are some options worth considering:

Davidson's Mill Pond Park, Riva Avenue, South Brunswick

John A. Phillips Open Space Preserve, Pleasant Valley Road, Old Bridge

John A. Phillips Park, Maple Street, Old Bridge

Tamarack Hollow Preserve, Hillcrest Avenue and Albrecht Lane, East Brunswick

Thompson Park Conservation Area, Prospect Plains Road, Monroe Township

For more info visit co.middlesex.nj.us/parksrecreation/davidson.asp.

Parsonage Rd. in Edison Township), and the **Stephen J. Capestro Amphithe-ater** in Roosevelt Park. The theater is the host to Plays-in-the-Park (1 Pine Dr., Edison; 732-548-2884), an effort dating back to the 1960s that brings Broadway-caliber musicals and performances to Middlesex County. Once reserved for the summer only, these shows are now a year-round happening. Each summer, visitors can take in 3 musicals amid Mother Nature, while the fall calls for an indoor performance of a children's musical. Meanwhile, in the winter, the community puts *Joseph and the Amazing Technicolor Dreamcoat* on stage at the State Theater in New Brunswick every year.

Where to Eat

The Frog and the Peach Restaurant. 29 Dennis St. at Hiram Square, New Brunswick; (732) 846-3216; frogandpeach.com. Open for lunch Mon through Fri from 11:30 a.m. to 2:30 p.m., and for dinner Mon through Thurs from 5:30 to 9:30 p.m., Fri and Sat from 5:30 to 10 p.m., and Sun from 4:30 to 9 p.m. This children's menu features apple slices and cheddar cheese as a starter and broiled scallops as a main course. $$

Gusto Grill. 1050 Rte. 18 North, East Brunswick; (732) 651-2737; gustogrill.com. Open Mon through Thurs from 4 p.m. to midnight, Fri and Sat from noon to 1 a.m., and Sun from noon to midnight. Even the pizza and burgers are fancy at this joint. It's the perfect place for families that enjoy a little adventure in their food. $$$

Ria Mar Restaurant & Bar. 25 Whitehead Ave., South River; (732) 257-1100; ria-mar .com. Open for lunch and dinner. Portuguese food at its best is what this restaurant promises to deliver with dishes, such as chicken in rice Portuguese style, and filet mignon medallions madrilena style. $$

Sunny Palace. 1069 Rte. 18 South, East Brunswick; (732) 651-8668; sunnypalace .com. Open Mon through Thurs from 11:30 a.m. to 10 p.m., Fri and Sat from 11:30 a.m. to 11 p.m., and Sun from 11 a.m. to 10 p.m. This is the place for Chinese food, including Hong Kong dim sum and a slew of interesting menu items, such as treasure winter melon soup. $$–$$$

Where to Stay

Best Western East Brunswick Inn. 764 Rte. 18, East Brunswick; (732) 238-4900; bestwestern.com. Newly updated rooms include a microwave and fridge. $$

Comfort Suites. 555 Old Bridge Tpke., East Brunswick; (732) 967-1505; comfort suites.com. The family will appreciate the **free** hot breakfast featuring eggs, yogurt, and more. $$

The Heldrich. 10 Livingston Ave., New Brunswick; (732) 729-4670; theheldrich.com. It counts concierge service among its best assets. $$

Hilton East Brunswick & Executive Center. 3 Tower Center Blvd., East Brunswick; (732) 828-2800; hilton.com. Family packages, cribs, high chairs, and a children's menu make this hotel a practical choice for families with little ones. $$$

Holiday Inn Express. 4 Tower Center Blvd., East Brunswick; (732) 247-6800; hiexpress .com. The vicinity to Six Flags Great Adventure and Princeton University means the chance for fantastic day trips, and the hotel's location right off the Turnpike makes it a convenient place to stay for those on a road trip. $

Sheraton Edison Hotel Raritan Center. 125 Raritan Center Pkwy., Edison; (732) 225-8300; starwoodhotels.com/sheraton. Newly renovated and fresh looking, the 267 rooms feature flat-panel HD TVs. $$

Monmouth County

W hile there's plenty of history in Monmouth County, its real draw is its place as the gateway to the Jersey Shore. There's Belmar with its family-friendly waters and Avon-by-the-Sea with its Victorian boardwalks and famous swans (on the quiet Sylvan Lake). There's Asbury Park, where musicians like Bruce "the Boss" Springsteen, Bon Jovi, and Southside Johnny and the Asbury Jukes launched their careers, and Long Branch, which once attracted many a VIP, including First Lady Mary Lincoln and eight US presidents. Today, families are still drawn to the county, and all it offers—from the legendary Monmouth Racetrack to the stately and historic lighthouses.

FunTime America (ages 5 and up)

111 Rte. 35, Cliffwood; (732) 583-4600; funtimeamerica.com. Open Mon through Wed from noon to 9 p.m., Thurs from noon to 10 p.m., Fri from noon to 11 p.m., Sat from 10 a.m. to midnight, and Sun from 10 a.m. to 10 p.m. Prices vary depending on the attraction and event in which you participate.

An indoor amusement park, FunTime America features attractions for kids of all ages. Little ones can tumble through a maze made just for them or hop aboard a train ride. Older kids can try to climb to the top of the rock wall or compete against one another in laser tag. Arcade games and a motion simulator round out the offerings. A section devoted to science has children visiting small exotic animals, such as boas and iguanas, and an arts and crafts center allows you the chance to build a friend much the same way kids do at Build-A-Bear stores. The party rooms—including one exclusively for princess parties—are great for groups looking to celebrate in privacy. Can you say "family reunion"?

Gateway National Recreation Area— Sandy Hook Unit (all ages)

1 Bay Ave., Highlands; nps.gov/gate. Open Apr through Oct from 5 a.m. to 10 p.m. and from Nov through Mar from 5 a.m. to 8 p.m. Admission is free, but from Memorial Day through Labor Day, you must pay a $10 beach parking fee from 7 a.m. to 4 p.m.

Part of the vast Gateway National Recreation Area, which also extends into three boroughs of New York, the Sandy Hook Unit in New Jersey is a veritable feast for history buffs and nature lovers alike. At the northern tip of the Jersey Shore, Sandy Hook is 2,044 acres of beach peninsula. Ocean beaches, salt marshes, and a maritime holly forest are the highlight of Sandy Hook. They provide the perfect atmosphere for families to enjoy swimming, fishing, biking, hiking, birding, camping, and boating. You could also simply picnic and lounge on the sand.

Beyond the natural wonder of Sandy Hook lies its special place in history. For starters, it is the home of the **Sandy Hook Lighthouse,** which is the oldest surviving lighthouse in the US. Lit for the first time in 1764 and built for New York merchants seeking to protect their ships, the lighthouse was occupied by British soldiers during the Revolution and was a sanctuary to those who sympathized with the king. Not surprisingly, the patriots pelted the place with cannons. It survived, and today you can tour the grounds. Now used as office space and a gift shop, the nearby **Lighthouse Keeper's Quarters** is also a historic building. Although it was built in the 1800s, its restoration reflects how it looked in the 1930s. It's worth checking out if you're in the area as it is also the place to go for lighthouse tour information.

The History House, an 1898 lieutenant's home that sits on Officer's Row and features 1940s furnishings, and the New Jersey Audubon Society's **Sandy Hook Bird Observatory** are charming abodes to check out. Those interested in the military will appreciate the **Nike Missile Radar,** which was charged with guiding nuclear missiles during the Cold War. A tour of this site promises to reveal what it must be like to stand the nuclear missiles up and, with a finger on the switch, await further orders. Although the Fort Hancock Museum is undergoing a renovation, you can walk the area to see the Battery Potter, a disappearing gun battery that was obsolete by the time it was built because of its slow speed, and the Battery John Gunnison, a rapid-fire disappearing gun battery.

Horse Park of New Jersey (all ages)

Route 524, Allentown; (609) 259-0170; horseparkofnewjersey.com. Check website for schedule and fees.

A visit to the Horse Park of New Jersey means seeing equine events at New Jersey's first major horse-show grounds. In addition to witnessing polo matches, water jumps, and elegant horses, you can also check out the special events on the grounds, like a recent barn dance and the annual Turkey Trot.

iPlay America (ages 5 and up)

110 Schanck Rd., Freehold; (732) 577-8200; iplayamerica.com. Open year-round, but you must check the website for hours because they change seasonally. Prices vary based on the attractions you take advantage of.

This new indoor theme park features everything from laser tag to go-karts. A Boardwalk Arcade will have you playing the latest arcade games. Attractions include mini bowling, bumper cars, and a 4-D theater. Experience the sensation of free flight on the Kite Flyer and a launch into the air on the Happy Swing. And try your hand at traditional boardwalk games, including the Shooting Gallery, Balloon Pop, and Whac-a-Mole.

Keansburg Amusement Park & Runaway Rapids Waterpark (all ages)

Laurel Avenue, Keansburg; (732) 495-1400; keansburgamusementpark.com. Open from Mar through Oct, but hours vary by season, so check the website. Prices vary depending on the attractions you visit.

With everything from a merry-go-round and bumper cars to the Double Shot, a 100-foot thrill ride that blasts riders up before dropping them back down, and the gravity-defying Gravitron, Keansburg Amusement Park offers something for everyone. One of the highlights for younger children is the mini train, which uses real gasoline to take children in the train around a miniature track. The Fast Trax Go-Karts is a draw for everyone, thanks to its two tracks—one for adults that encourages friendly competition and another for kids that features smaller cars and careful supervision. Unlike most of today's amusement parks, Keansburg charges visitors per ride, so you can spend what you want by carefully picking and choosing the attractions to fill your day. In addition to rides, you can play carnival games, including one that still costs only 10 cents.

Light Up My Life:
New Jersey's Lighthouses

New Jersey is home to 11 lighthouses that have been guiding mariners in the Atlantic Ocean and its surrounding waters for more than 100 years. The US's oldest surviving lighthouse, the Sandy Hook Lighthouse, calls New Jersey home, too. Here is a list of the others you might want to visit:

Absecon Lighthouse, 31 S. Rhode Island Ave., Atlantic City; (609) 449-1919; absteconlighthouse.org. The state's tallest lighthouse is also the country's third tallest and one of its oldest lighthouses. After climbing the 228 steps to the top, you can train your eye on both the spectacular AC skyline and the original Fresnel lens, which was first lit in 1857.

Barnegat Lighthouse, Barnegat Light; (609) 494-2016; state.nj.us/dep/parksandforests. This lighthouse was considered a hero to those guiding vessels at this "change of course" point, a dangerous section of the shoreline.

Cape May Lighthouse, Cape May Point; (609) 884-2159; state.nj.us/dep/parksandforests. Cape May Lighthouse is beautiful on its own, but it also happens to be a nice place to view the fall bird migration.

East Point Lighthouse, End of E. Point Road at the mouth of the Maurice River; (856) 785-1120; lighthousefriends.com. Open to tours infrequently, the exterior of the East Point Lighthouse has been restored, but a lack of funds has prevented a renovation of the interior. Still, a brick oil house is eye-catching.

Finns Point Rear Range Light, Fort Mott Road to Lighthouse Road, Supawna Meadows Wildlife Refuge; lighthousefriends.com. Made of wrought iron, which was delivered to the construction site by mule, this is not your average lighthouse. Its metal exterior and build has one thinking more water tower than lighthouse. There are no tours of this lighthouse, but it is worth passing by.

Hereford Inlet Lighthouse, Central Avenue, North Wildwood; (609) 522-4520; herefordlighthouse.org. More than a historic lighthouse, this one is a museum and is also surrounded by gardens with hundreds of varieties of plants for visitors to explore and admire.

Sea Girt Lighthouse, Beacon Boulevard and Ocean Avenue, Sea Girt; (732) 974-0514; seagirtlighthouse.com. Poorly constructed, many believed this lighthouse would crash into the sea. As a result, in 1921, it became the first Jersey Shore lighthouse to have a radio fog signal.

Tinicum Rear Range Lighthouse, 2nd Street and Mantua Avenue, Paulsboro; tinicumrearrangelighthouse.org. Having a more industrial look than traditional lighthouses, the Tinicum Rear Range Lighthouse is billed as having guided Delaware River commerce for more than 125 years. Today the site can be used for celebrations, even weddings.

Tucker's Island Lighthouse, 120 W. Main St., Tuckerton; (609) 296-8868; tuckertonseaport.org/index.html. Rendered useless by Absecon Lighthouse, this lighthouse was plagued from the start. In fact, it was almost washed away and its remains burned. In 2000, a recreation of the lighthouse was built to commemorate the island and lighthouse that once was. Today visitors can see exhibits about New Jersey's lighthouses here.

Twin Lights of Navesink, Lighthouse Road, Highlands; (732) 872-1814; twin-lights.org/home.htm. Once known as the best and brightest light in North America, the Twin Lights overlook the Shrewsbury River, Sandy Hook, Raritan Bay, and the Atlantic Ocean, with the New York skyline as a backdrop.

At **Runaway Rapids Waterpark,** you also pay per ride rather than footing the bill for general admission. The water park aims to please children and adults alike with a range of rides and attractions that should appeal to them both. There are 18 water slides of varying heights and speeds, so you can choose the ones you are most comfortable using. A kiddie lagoon area, toddler play zone, and lazy river round out the family friendly offerings. Spa pools and lounge chairs can help mom and dad relax while the kids frolic.

Lakewood BlueClaws (ages 5 and up)

2 Stadium Way, Lakewood Township; (732) 901-7000; milb.com. Season is from Apr through Oct. Tickets cost $10 for adults; $7 for juniors, seniors, and military; and free for children under 4; general admission lawn tickets cost $7.
South Atlantic League Champions in 2006, 2009, and 2010, the Lakewood Blue-Claws make minor league baseball exciting. In the franchise's 10 years playing in Lakewood Township, it has also produced big leaguers, including 2008 World Series MVP Cole Hamels and Phillies starting catcher Carlos Ruiz. Recently, the team retired number 29 in honor of former BlueClaws player and current Phillies slugger Ryan Howard, who also rehabbed with the team.

Should you come to a game, you will find yourself in a relatively new stadium—**FirstEnergy Park** was built in 2001—with lots of amenities, including 20 luxury suites, 2 party decks, 3 picnic areas, and a full video scoreboard. If you are going to be in the area in the summer months and your 7- to 12-year-old child aspires to be a slugger, you can sign him or her up for the team's 4-day youth training camps. The best part is that the current BlueClaws themselves provide the professional instruction. Although there are all sorts of events happening at the stadium, you might just want to take your family out to the ballpark for some old-fashioned fun—watching a baseball game.

Metz Bicycle Museum (ages 5 and up)

54 W. Main St. (rear), Freehold; (732) 462-7363; metzbicyclemuseum.com. Open by appointment only. Admission costs $10 for adults and $5 for children under 12.
Freehold native and retired businessman David Metz shares his collection of antiques with the world at this museum. The focus, of course, is bicycles. A trip to the museum will have you checking out everything from an 8-foot lamplighter bicycle that was ridden in the 1890s to light gas street lamps in New York City, to trick bicycles that have been used in circuses and other performances. A local gem is the star of the museum: The 1896 "Zimmy" bicycle comes from the

Freehold bicycle factory owned by the town's own Arthur Zimmerman, who was the world's first bicycle racing champion. The showcase at the museum also includes bicycle accessories—from horns to seats—children's riding toys, kitchen gadgets, pencil sharpeners, cast iron bottle openers (some in the shape of birds), antique cars, and even antique mousetraps. Metz himself is a character. Once a farmer, he takes an interest in all gadgets and has appeared on his bicycle in parades, including the Macy's Thanksgiving Day Parade and the Main Street parade at Disney World.

Monmouth Battlefield State Park (all ages)

347 Freehold-Englishtown Rd., Manalapan; (732) 462-9616; state.nj.us/dep/parks andforests/parks/monbat.html. Open daily from 8 a.m. to 4:30 p.m. Admission is **free** for all, but there are fees associated with some activities, such as boat launching.

As the site of the Battle of Monmouth Courthouse, one of the largest of the American Revolution, Monmouth Battlefield State Park offers more than your average park. Every year in late June, actors in period costumes reenact the battle. You might pass by enlisted men or women cooking, mending, and washing. The recruiting sergeant often has children drill with wooden muskets.

More than a battlefield, the site also provides a view on nature. A refreshing walk through the trails is a charming way to pass the day. The family farms in the area cultivate soybeans, corn, and apple, peach, and nectarine orchards. The orchard run by the Applegate family provides a pick-your-own farm. The months from the spring through the fall bring a different kind of produce to the forefront—strawberries in May, pie cherries in June, peaches and nectarines in mid- to late July, apples in September, and pumpkins in October. On your stroll you might also bump right into exhibits on Perrine Hill, Combs Hill, and the Hedgerow that explain the battle. Although the buildings are closed, you can also check out Craig House, the farmhouse that belonged to the Craig family. The highlight is its 1746 kitchen. Imagine cooking there!

Poricy Park Conservancy (ages 5 and up)

345 Oak Hill Rd., Middletown; (732) 842-5966; poricypark.org/home.html. Trails are open from dawn to 10 p.m.; the Nature Center is open Mon through Fri from 9 a.m. to 4 p.m.; farmhouse is open from 3 to 4 p.m. on the last Sun of the month. The fossil beds are open Apr through Oct from dawn to dusk. Rentals for fossil exploration cost $5 plus a refundable $5 deposit; community fossil digs cost $8 per person or $32 for a family (2 adults, 3 children).

On 250 acres of open space, Poricy Park Conservancy offers visitors the chance to see wildlife in their natural habitat, visit the Murray Farmhouse, and investigate prehistoric fossil beds. A walk around the park will also reveal the colonial garden featuring sweet corn, peas, beans, and carrots, at the Murray farmstead. The idea was to create a garden similar to what the Murrays would have had in their home garden in the late 1700s and early 1800s.

The **Murray Farmhouse** and barn are typical of the kinds of dwellings that attracted middle class families of the time. Both still sit on their original foundations despite having been restored. The historical significance of the home and barn was unknown even after the town purchased them. It wasn't until 1973 when general repairs were being done, that research was discovered that proved the home was from the colonial era.

While the home and barn date back to America's birth, the area surrounding them goes all the way back to prehistoric times. You and your family can dig for treasures dating from when dinosaurs roamed the Earth. The fossils found on-site date back to the Cretaceous period of the Mesozoic era. At that time, Poricy Park was a shallow ocean. The harder parts of ocean animals—think teeth, bones, and shells—were preserved. Most of the fossils found in Poricy Park are shellfish. Families are welcome to rent equipment or join community digs to

explore the area for more fossils. You must follow careful instructions, which are available at the park's website. But the kids will love putting on their paleontologist hats and digging up history.

Silverball Museum Arcade (all ages)

1000 Ocean Ave., Asbury Park; (732) 774-4994; silverballmuseum.com. Open Mon through Thurs from 11 a.m. to 9 p.m., Fri from 11 a.m. to 1 a.m., Sat from 10 a.m. to 1 a.m., and Sun from 10 a.m. to 9 p.m. $20 for a daily re-entry pass, $10 for 2-hour pass, $7.50 for an express pass of 30 minutes or less, **free** for kids under 5 (who are there with a paying adult).

For the chance to see and play with pinball machines from as far back as 1933, visit the Silverball Museum Arcade. With pinball machines ranging from the 1956 Candy Wheel, which was considered one of the best baseball games of its era, to the 1976 Surf Champ, where the goal is to complete all 11 numbers in any sequence, you can lose an entire day trying to become the next pinball wizard. When hunger strikes, you can sample lobster rolls, pulled pork, funnel cake, or even *tartufo* on a stick.

Six Flags Great Adventure & Wild Safari (all ages)

1 Six Flags Blvd., Jackson; (732) 928-1821; sixflags.com/greatAdventure. Open Apr through Oct. General admission costs $59.99, $36.99 for those under 54 inches tall, **free** for ages 2 and under; safari upgrade with theme park ticket costs $11.99.

The biggest Six Flags amusement park in the country is in Jackson, NJ. From Apr through Oct, visitors can seek adventure on thrill rides, munch on snacks, and pose for photos with characters such as Bugs Bunny. The Big Wheel, a 15-story, ecofriendly Ferris wheel; go-kart racing; and a rock wall for climbing are among the activities. Little ones will enjoy the carousel, Daffy Duck's hot air balloons, and the Bugs Bunny Fun Factory play area. On those steamy days, they can cool off at Bugs Bunny National Park Water Tower, a sprinkling fountain. For a bit more adventure, the family can drive through the Wild Safari, which is home to 1,200 exotic animals. Animals, such as brown bears, giraffes, lions, and kangaroos, walk around the safari and can come close to your car as you drive through. You can find a slew of food options at the park, even hand-rolled sushi and chicken fritters.

Where to Eat

Bahrs Landing. 2 Bay Ave., Highlands/Sandy Hook; (732) 872-1245; bahrslanding
.com. Hours vary by season, so call ahead or check the website. In business since
1917, this family-run seafood restaurant features kiddie cocktails and lobster on its
children's menu. $$$

Jakes Crab Shack. 500 Ocean Ave. (on the boardwalk), Belmar; (732) 894-3502;
jakescrabshack.com. Open for breakfast, lunch, and dinner. Italian hot dogs with pep-
pers and onions and crab cake sandwiches are among the highlights at this affordable
eatery. $

Lamberti's Cucina Manalapan. Galleria Shopping Center, 100 Rte. 9 North,
Manalapan; (732) 431-2014; lambertis.com. Open Mon through Fri from 11:30 a.m. to
10 p.m., Sat from noon to 10 p.m., and Sun from 1 to 9 p.m. Simple Italian cuisine is
sure to satisfy even the pickiest eaters. $$

10th Ave Burrito. 817 Belmar Plaza, Belmar; (732) 280-1515; tenthaveburrito.com.
Open Mon through Sat 11 a.m. to 9 p.m., and Sun from 11 a.m. to 8 p.m. Everything
at this dine-in or take-out restaurant is made from scratch, and you can even have
your burritos delivered to you at the beach. The Mexican fare was featured on the
Food Network's *Diners, Drive-Ins and Dives*. $

Where to Stay

The Berkeley Oceanfront Hotel. 1401 Ocean Ave., Asbury Park; (732) 776-6700;
berkeleyhotelnj.com. Asbury Park is for families that want to rock out, and this hotel,
which is close to the city's boardwalk, is a sophisticated place to kick up your feet
when the band is done playing. $$

Comfort Inn Middletown-Red Bank. 750 Rte. 35 South, Middletown; (877) 424-
6423; middletowncomfortinn.com. **Free** hot breakfast, an outdoor heated pool,
and an Outback Steakhouse on premises are among the amenities families might
like. $$

Holiday Inn Hazlet. 2870 Rte. 35, Hazlet; (877) 834-3613; holidayinn.com. Billing itself as a family-oriented hotel, the Holiday Inn Hazlet is close to Keansburg Amusement Park and the Monmouth Mall. $$

Ocean Place Resort & Spa. 1 Ocean Blvd., Long Branch; (732) 571-4000 or (800) 411-6493; oceanplace.com. A palace on the Jersey Shore, this luxurious hotel and spa promises something for everyone in the family. $$$$

Sheraton Eatontown Hotel. 6 Industrial Way East, Eatontown; (732) 542-6500 or (800) 325-3535; sheratoneatontown.com. Its proximity to New York, Philadelphia, and the Jersey Shore, including Atlantic City and Seaside Heights, combined with its brand name, build confidence in guests. $$–$$$

Burlington County

Burlington County is the largest county in size in New Jersey, but only about 448,730 people live there. An agriculture epicenter, Burlington County has more acres devoted to farming than any other in the state. The highlight of the harvest is its plump, juicy blueberries. In fact, they are said to be the largest blueberries in the world. It is also the second largest producer of cranberries in the country. While tasting the county's sweet berries is a must-do, there's also a bit of history worth visiting.

Historic Smithville Park (all ages)

801 Smithville Rd., Mount Holly; (609) 265-5858; smithvilleconservancy.org. Call ahead for hours and prices.

Smithville was a company town that was ahead of its time. Worker's rights, sustainability, and town planning were top priorities for this industrial plant known for its woodworking machinery, bicycle railroad, and high-wheeled bicycle. On a self-guided tour, you can check out the stairway to the bowling alley, factory complex, and ruins of the gristmill, dairy barn, and sheds in addition to other landmarks from Smithville's past. A walk around also reveals nature's gifts. Specifically, you might spot a white-tailed deer, wild turkey, red fox, beaver, rabbit, red-tailed hawk, great blue heron, or waterfowl. In addition to the historic industrial village and the wildlife, you can also hike, bike, or even ride a horse on the trails. The 600-foot floating trail on Smithville Lake is a chance for fun on the water. Rancocas Creek and Smithville Lake offer canoeing and fishing opportunities. A butterfly garden is a wonderful place to chill out with the family—and spy the fairest insect of them all.

Nature **at its Best**

Burlington County is wealthy in open spaces filled with natural wonders. Here are some of the best places from which you can explore the bounty:

Amico Island Park, Norman Avenue, Delran Township. This is best for its river view and wildlife, including red foxes and cottontail rabbits.

Boundary Creek Natural Resource Area, Creek Road, Moorestown Township. Birding and a butterfly and hummingbird garden set this park apart from the others.

Crystal Lake Park, off Axe Factory Road, Crystal Lake. Hiking, biking, fishing, and horseback riding attract visitors to this park.

Long Bridge Park, Deacon Road, Hainesport Township. A forested sanctuary on Rancocas Creek, Long Bridge Park has a Zen-like feel and gives visitors the chance to hike, bike, and picnic.

Pennington Park, Creek Road, Delanco Township. A visit to Pennington Park is like walking into a science book because you can observe forests, wetlands, a tidal pond, marshland, creek, shoreline, and a diverse collection of terrain.

For more information, visit co.burlington.nj.us.

Where to Eat

Forno Pizzeria & Grille. 28 Church Rd., Maple Shade; (856) 608-7711; fornopizzeria .com. Open Mon through Thurs from 11 a.m. to 10 p.m., Fri and Sat from 11 a.m. to 10 p.m., and Sun from noon to 9 p.m. Gourmet pizza and homemade pasta make this restaurant one to which you'll want to return. Stuffed shells are the kind of item that makes the kid's menu shine. $

Robin's Nest Restaurant. 2 Washington St., Mount Holly; (609) 261-6149; robins nestmountholly.com. Open Mon through Sat for lunch from 11 a.m. to 2:30 p.m.; open for dinner Tues from 4:30 to 8 p.m., Wed and Thurs from 4:30 p.m. to 9 p.m., Fri from 4:30 p.m. to 9:30 p.m., Sat from 5 to 9:30 p.m., open Sun for brunch from 10 a.m. to 2 p.m. Honey pecan chicken and ginger salmon are among the dishes at this French-American restaurant. And flatbread pizza and soup and salad are options for the kids. $$

Where to Stay

Courtyard Mount Laurel. 1000 Century Pkwy., Mount Laurel; (856) 273-4400. Healthy dining options and airport updates via the GoBoard make this a practical choice for families. $$

DoubleTree Suites by Hilton Hotel Mt. Laurel. 515 Fellowship Rd. North, Mount Laurel; (856) 778-8999; doubletree1.hilton.com. A living room and Crabtree & Evelyn bath products are great perks at this hotel. $$

Hampton Inn Philadelphia/Mt. Laurel. 5000 Crawford Place, Mount Laurel; (856) 778-5535; hamptoninn1.hilton.com. There are 126 rooms in this conveniently located and affordable hotel for families. $

Hyatt Place. 8000 Crawford Place, Mount Laurel; (856) 840-0770; mtlaurel.place .hyatt.com. The benefit of staying here is that you can just as easily visit Philadelphia as you can all the attractions in Burlington County. $$

The Westin Mount Laurel. 555 Fellowship Rd., Mount Laurel; (856) 778-7300; star woodhotels.com/westin. A beautiful, modern design draws guests to this property. $$

Ocean County

The second largest county in the state, Ocean County is proudest of its 638 miles of pine barrens and barrier islands and 45-mile coastline along the Atlantic Ocean. Because it's such a lovely place to retire, senior citizens make up a lot of the population, which stands at more than 576,560 people. Who wouldn't want to spend their golden years within walking distance of the beach? Still, young people make the journey to this county every summer with the hopes of finding love in the sand and working on their tan. (C'mon this is Jersey, home of the bronze gods and goddesses!) Your kids will have fun here, too, thanks to the boardwalk rides that are just for them and a chance at building sandcastles and catching waves.

Blackbeard's Cave (all ages)

136 Rte. 9, Bayville; (732) 286-4414; blackbeardscave.com. Open year-round but outdoor activities are limited in the colder weather. Outdoor rides and amusements are open from March through the first week in November while the restaurant, driving range, and arcade are open all year. Admission is free but you pay for the various activities available. Children's rides cost from 1 to 4 tickets, and tickets are 75 cents each, minigolf, go-karts are 8 tickets or $6. You can purchase a book of 45 tickets for $30 or two books, which come with a free go kart ride. Tickets are good for the entire season. Baseball tokens are $1 each, 12 pitches per token, Driving range buckets come in three sizes and price points: $5, $7, and $9. $–$$$.

An amusement park, Blackbeard's Cave features minigolf, ponies, go-karts, bumper boats, batting and driving cages, an archery range, laser tag, remote boats,

Schoolhouses **Rock**

New Jersey is full of historic schoolhouses and schoolhouse museums. Clearly, education has been in style since the state was born. Rather than telling the story of grandparents walking 20 miles in the snow and sleet to get to school, show your kids what it was like to learn in one room with not much more than your teacher. Here are some schoolhouses worth visiting:

Giffordtown Schoolhouse Museum, Leitz Boulevard and Wisteria Lane, Tuckerton; (609) 296-2394; tuckertonlehhs.org/schoolhouse .php. In the 1885, two-room Giffordtown Schoolhouse, you will now discover a model of the Tuckerton Wireless Tower and artifacts from the Quakers.

Lacey Schoolhouse Museum, 126 S. Main St., Forked River; (609) 971-0467; ocean.nj.us/museums/Lacey/about.htm. Built in 1868 and used until 1952, the schoolhouse is now a museum featuring tools, utensils, and photos from the past.

and arcade. To cool off on those humid days, you can participate in the Water Wars, a battle that will have you catapulting water balloons at friends and family. Make like an American gladiator and challenge your buddy to a good ol' joust, using those big foam weapons. Lollipop swings and a canoe ride make the kiddie zone exciting for the little ones. And a climbing wall will challenge the older members of the family.

Double Trouble State Park (all ages)
581 Pinewald Keswick Rd., Bayville; (732) 341-6662; nj.gov/dep/parksandforests. Open daily from 8 a.m. to dusk; office is open Wed through Sun. Admission is free for all.

Double Trouble State Park, despite its name, is the opposite of trouble. It's a lovely place where visitors can learn about the Pine Barrens and New Jersey's cranberry bogs. You can even plan your trip around the cranberry harvest if that is something you would like to see. Hunting and hiking are also popular pastimes

Old Monroe Stone Schoolhouse, 410–412 Rte. 94 (North Church Road), Hardyston Township; hardystonheritage.org. Get a glimpse at a hand-hewn stone building that was used as a school from 1819 to about 1926.

South Branch School House, 2120 S. Branch Rd., Branchburg; (908) 526-1300; visitsomersetnj.org/play/historic-sites. A prime example of Victorian Italianate schools, which is a popular design in New Jersey, the Little Red School House was built in 1873, and it is striking. Besides its red color, it is charming and exactly what you'd imagine an old schoolhouse to be. It retains almost all its original exterior and interior. It will give you the chance to show your children what school was like for kids in the late 1800s.

Wescott Preserve, 1020 Rte. 31, Lebanon; (908) 782-1158; co.hunt erdon.nj.us. As part of the 15-acre county park, the John Reading School or District Schoolhouse #97 was constructed in 1861. But a school is said to have been on the site since 1796.

at the park. For something different entirely, you can walk through the historic village, a complete company town. These villages were typical of others once in the area that were isolated and completely reliant on the success of a particular industry. There's a restored sawmill and a cranberry sorting and packing plant with nearly intact equipment. Although the community revolved around those two buildings, which brought work to the people, there was also a schoolhouse, general store, pickers' cottages, and foreman's house. The tea-stained Cedar Creek, which gets its color from the tannic acid in the roots of the cedars lining the creek, provides the water necessary for the cranberry bogs. Although there are no rentals on-site, you can canoe and kayak in the creek, but tubing, rafting, and swimming are prohibited.

Fantasy Island Amusement Park (all ages)

320 7th St., Beach Haven; (609) 492-4000; fantasyislandpark.com. Park is open May through Sept from 6 p.m. to closing (which happens between 11 p.m. and

midnight); arcade is open year-round, but check website for hours. Prices vary depending on rides and games in which you partake; on POP (Pay One Price) days, pay $17 for all rides from 2 to 7 p.m.

This is the ideal place for families looking for old-fashioned fun in a modern setting. One of the highlights of the park is the Family Casino, which has people of all ages playing the slots and other games to earn credit for prizes as opposed to winning and losing cash. Carnival games and rides that range from little boats for little kids to a giant Ferris wheel for big kids make up the crux of the park's offerings. But there's also entertainment. You can take in a concert by a local band or meet Ben Franklin and Betsy Ross, who talk history and do magic tricks for the crowd.

Island Beach State Park (all ages)

Seaside Park; (732) 793-0506; nj.gov/dep/parksandforests. Open daily sunrise to sunset. From Memorial Day through Labor Day, entrance fees are charged per vehicle: $6 on weekdays and $10 on weekends.

One of the state's last significant barrier island ecosystems, Island Beach Park is a treasure. It is also one of the few undeveloped barrier beaches on the northern Atlantic coast. Extending for 10 miles between the Atlantic Ocean and Barnegat Bay, Island Beach State Park gives visitors the chance to see primary dunes, thicket, freshwater wetlands, maritime forest, and tidal marshes, along with osprey, peregrine falcons, wading birds, shorebirds, waterfowl, and songbirds. Swimmers and surfers alike enjoy the beach.

The Island Beach Northern and Southern Natural Areas are the barrier beaches that remain untouched. Portions of the northern section are restricted to protect it. Sand dunes, salt-sculptured vegetation, green salt marshes, and the maritime forest are among the wonders you can observe. Fishing, swimming, surfing, sailboarding, and even horseback riding happen in the rest of the park and beach area. Canoe and kayak tours are available through the **Sedge Island Marine Conservation Zone** of highly productive tidal marshes, creeks, ponds, and open water. You can also see a collection of 400 plants that have been classified and preserved at the **Emily DeCamp Interpretive Center.**

Jenkinson's Aquarium (all ages)

Boardwalk, 300 Ocean Ave., Point Pleasant Beach; (732) 892-0600; jenkinsons .com/aquarium. Open Mon through Fri from 9:30 a.m. to 5 p.m., and Sat and Sun

from 10 a.m. to 5 p.m. Admission costs $10 for adults, $6 for children ages 3 to 12 and seniors, and free for children ages 2 and under.

A charming aquarium on the Point Pleasant Beach Boardwalk, Jenkinson's Aquarium is an educational place to take the kids when they start to get bored in the sand. Within an hour, you can see all the exhibits. But you might find yourself staying longer because the kids will want to linger over one of the feeding-time demonstrations. At the aquarium, you can watch trainers feed penguins, sharks, seals, and American alligators. For children who are truly interested in marine biology, summer camp at the aquarium is a great option. Children ages 11 to 16 can sign up for a day working as junior keepers. It's a chance to work alongside staff and assist with various tasks related to the animals' care. For kids ages 5 to 10, a weeklong camp has them learning about different animals in the aquarium, making crafts, and playing games. Each session has a different theme, such as "Explore the Deep" and "Rainforest Romp."

Long Beach Island Museum (ages 6 and up)

Engleside and Beach Avenues, Beach Haven; (609) 492-0700; lbimuseum.org. Open in the summer 7 days a week from 10 a.m. to 4 p.m., and from the end of June through the beginning of Sept on Wed evening from 7 to 9 p.m.; open spring and fall weekends. Admission donation is $3.

Housed in what was an Episcopal church built in 1882, the Long Beach Island Historical Association tries to share the community's history with visitors to the museum. The museum's highlights include exhibits on shipwrecks and walking ghost tours. Special events, such as a Trash & Treasure sale, wedding road show, and porch party, take place at the museum throughout the summer.

Popcorn Park Zoo (all ages)

Humane Way at Lacey Road, Forked River; (609) 693-1900; ahscares.org. Open 11 a.m. to 5 p.m. 7 days a week, and from 11 a.m. to 2 p.m. on holidays. Admission costs $5 for adults, $4 for seniors and children, free for children under 3.

Popcorn Park Zoo was born of good deeds. The zoo was developed in 1977 to house abandoned, injured, ill, exploited, abused, or elderly wildlife, exotic and farm animals, and birds. On 7 acres in the middle of the state's Pine Barrens, this zoo is a sanctuary to which you're all invited. You will encounter a wide range of animals from Australian wallabies to African lions. There's a monkey house, reptile house, and farm animals, such as horses, pigs, and sheep. As you walk through the zoo, you will learn the story of each animal and discover what

Beaches **of Ocean County**

In Jersey, people go "down the Shore," and the major shore points—
or at least the ones made popular on reality TV—are in Ocean
County. So, pump your fists, wear your hair high as can be, and get
your tan on (with the proper sun protection, of course). Here are a
few beaches you could visit with your family:

Barnegat Light Beach
A family-friendly beach, Barnegat Light has only one flaw: You can't
bring food on the beach.

Beach Haven
Nearby playground and tennis courts provide additional entertainment when spending the day at the beach.

Lavallette
If you and the family enjoy surfing, then you should head to this
beach to catch some waves.

Long Beach Island
This town offers more than the beach. There's fishing, crabbing, and
clamming, the Pine Barrens, and a wildlife refuge.

brought him or her to this particular zoo. You may be moved to tears, but you
and your children will gain a new respect for Mother Nature and all its creatures.

Robert J. Novins Planetarium (all ages)
Ocean County College; (732) 255-0343; ocean.edu/campus/planetarium/Novins
GeneralInfo.htm. Check website for shows and times. Tickets cost $10 for adults,
$8 for seniors (ages 60 and over), and $7 for children (ages 12 and under) per
show.
The newly renovated Robert J. Novins Planetarium, which reopened in 2010,
gives families the chance to learn about the universe—especially its stars—in an
entertaining way. Shows that have you looking up at the ceiling in awe include
The Stars from My Backyard, which helps the youngest spectators understand

Point Pleasant Beach
One of the most entertaining beaches, Point Pleasant is great for finding shells in the sand and its boardwalk features rides, arcades, batting cages, and even Jenkinson's Aquarium.

Seaside Heights
Home of the *Jersey Shore* cast, this beach and boardwalk attracts young adults with an attitude by night, but during the day, you can take advantage of the attractions and the sun and sand.

Ship Bottom
Known as the gateway to Long Beach Island, this beach gets its name from its origins as the site of a shipwreck.

Surf City
In case you weren't sure, there's more surfing at this beach.

Windward Beach
Pack a picnic and head to Wayward Beach, where you can eat as long as you can clean up. Even barbecuing is permitted.

what kinds of stars they can track by just looking up at the sky in their own backyard, and *Laser Pink Floyd: The Wall,* which is a laser light show set to the music of the rock band. Shows don't usually last much more than an hour, which is the perfect length before the kids—not to mention you——get antsy.

Toms River Seaport Society & Maritime Museum

(ages 6 and up)
Northeast corner of Hooper Avenue and Water Street, Toms River; (732) 349-9209; tomsriverseaport.org. Open Tues, Thurs, and Sat from 10 a.m. to 2 p.m.
Like the rest of New Jersey, Ocean County is not without its history. Because of its vicinity to the ocean, this county's past is tied to a maritime heritage. The Toms River Seaport Society & Maritime Museum is charged with keeping alive

those traditions. Founded in 1976, the society opens its doors to the public so it can see firsthand what life on Barnegat Bay in New Jersey was like then and now. The museum, which is in a restored 1868 carriage house from the Joseph Francis estate, features ship models and small boat displays. Outside, you can imagine yourself setting sail on one of the wooden boats, and the restoration shop is a chance to look at the tools used on ships through the years and the painstaking restoration projects the group has taken on.

Tuckerton Seaport & Baymen's Museum
Working Maritime Village (all ages)

120 W. Main St., Tuckerton; (609) 296-8868; tuckertonseaport.org. Open daily from 10 a.m. to 5 p.m. Admission costs $8 for adults, $6 for seniors ages 62 and up, $3 for children ages 6 to 12, free for children 5 and under.

A maritime village along Tuckerton Creek, this seaport includes 17 recreated and historic buildings. There's a forest and wetlands for visitors to explore. Daily demonstrators—boat builders, carvers, and basket makers—give visitors a glimpse at the craftsmanship synonymous with the Jersey Shore. A recreated Tucker's Island Lighthouse is a great photo op, not to mention a chance to learn about privateers and pirates on the Jersey Shore (see "Light Up My Life: New Jersey's Lighthouses" on p. 88). And a tour of Tuckerton Creek on the *Wasting Time* charter boat is a leisurely way to take in the scene.

What many don't know about is the **Jacques Cousteau National Estuarine Research Reserve Interpretive Center.** Its *Life on the Edge* exhibit, which is housed in the Yacht Club, is managed by the Institute of Marine and Coastal Sciences of Rutgers University. It gives visitors an opportunity to better understand the Great Bay, Pinelands, Barrier Island, and Open Ocean ecosystems. The reserve encompasses the point where freshwater from the Mullica Bay and saltwater from the Atlantic Ocean meet in the Great Bay. The staff studies the area, conducts research, and educates the public.

Where to Eat

Capt'N Ed's Place. 1001 Arnold Ave., Point Pleasant; (732) 892-4121; captnedsplace.com. Open daily for dinner from 4:30 p.m. A Jersey Shore favorite, this is the place to feast on surf and turf, including steak on a stone. $$

Carousel Candies. Jenkinson's Boardwalk, Point Pleasant Beach. Open year-round. Pick up taffy, homemade fudge, and cookies. $–$$

Hemingway's Cafe. 612 Boulevard, Seaside Heights; (732) 830-1256; hemingways seaside.com. Open for lunch and dinner. Feast on everything from pasta to burgers at this restaurant, which also features live entertainment at times. $$

Klee's Bar and Grill. 101 Boulevard, Seaside Heights; (732) 830-1996; kleesbarand grill.com. Open year-round. Famous thin-crust pizza pies and juicy burgers are the draw at this local hangout. $–$$

Woodies Drive-In. 5th Street and Long Beach Island Boulevard, Ship Bottom; (609) 361-7300; woodiesburgers.com. Quality ingredients and fresh-cooked burgers, hot dogs, and fries keep people coming back to Woodies. The prices don't hurt either. $

Where to Stay

The Cast House. Ocean side of the Boulevard, Long Beach Island; call Dave at (609) 548-0800; lbinjvacations.com. Once used for the Surflight Theater's cast house, this home has been renovated to provide 10 bedrooms that have been decorated to represent different Broadway plays. For instance, in the Cinderella room, you will feel like a princess in an ornate bed and plush linens, whereas in the Oklahoma room, you will sleep in a bed that comes replete with giant wheels to look like a wagon. Prices available upon request.

White Pearl Hotel. 201 Summer Ave., Seaside Heights; (732) 830-4242; thewhite pearlhotel.com. An indoor pool and rooftop sundeck top the amenities at the White Pearl Hotel. Prices available upon request.

White Sands Oceanfront Resort & Spa. 1205 Ocean Ave., Point Pleasant Beach; (732) 899-3370 or (888) 558-8958; thewhitesands.com. Set on a private stretch of Point Pleasant Beach, White Sands is conveniently located near all the action. $$–$$$$

Southern New Jersey

Southern New Jersey

Camden County

C amden County grew to have a tradition of tolerance. Among the first Europeans to arrive in the county were the Quakers, a peaceful group that belonged to the Society of Friends and had been persecuted for their beliefs in England. Here they sought religious freedom, equitable taxes, and government representation. When the Revolutionary War took hold, the Quakers would not bear arms for either side due to their practice of nonviolence. Again, they faced some persecution, especially while the British occupied nearby Philadelphia. But they endured. In the 1800s, a railroad and a canal spurred business in the area, and it soon became an economic force. While the residents tried to stay out of the Revolutionary War, they participated on the side of the Union in the Civil War. Industry continued to flourish after the war was won, and Camden County lived by the phrase, "In Camden's supplies, the world relies." In fact, it is still home to The Campbell Soup Company, which maintains its headquarters in Camden today. A series of bridges helped link the county to Philadelphia, where many residents even today still work. Camden County also played a role in the arts. Poet Walt Whitman called Camden home, and his house and burial ground are still attractions for visitors to the area.

Camden Waterfront

The Camden Waterfront offers beautiful views of the Delaware River and the Philadelphia skyline. It supports the Camden GreenWay, a network of trails that you can find throughout the city and on which you can explore, hike, and bike, and the RiverLink Ferry, a double-decker ferry that allows visitors to cross the

Delaware River from May through September. And the Camden Waterfront also features other attractions that continue to provide fun for the family.

Here's what you can expect:

Adventure Aquarium

1 Aquarium Dr., Camden; (800) 616-JAWS; adventureaquarium.com. **Open year round from 10 a.m. to 5 p.m. $23.95 for adults, $17.95 for children ages 2 to 12,** free **for children under 2 with an accompanying adult. $$$–$$$$.**
Who isn't fascinated by the world under water? You can walk with sharks overhead or touch them, observe penguins 20 feet underwater, or take in the show that the seals put on all on their own. A 4-D theater allows visitors to view movies that make you feel as though you're right in the middle of them. Recent shows included *Cloudy with a Chance of Meatballs* and *Sea Monsters*.

Battleship *New Jersey*

1 Riverside Dr., Camden; (856) 966-1652; battleshipnewjersey.org. **Open from May to September daily from 9 a.m. to 5 p.m. Closed every January. In the winter, usually open on weekends only. Call ahead to be sure. $18.50 for adults, self-guided tours, $19.95 with a guide; $14 for children ages 6 to 11, seniors, and veterans for self-guided tours, $15 with a guide;** free **for children 5 and under and active duty military. $$$.**
Besides getting to say that you have walked aboard the US Navy's most-decorated battleship, the USS *New Jersey,* you can learn about the missions executed aboard ship and have a chance to try your hand at combat on the 4-D flight simulator, which has you flying and fighting aboard a Seahawk plane. There is even an overnight encampment program for those who want to live like a sailor by putting their stuff in the same lockers used by the Navy, sleeping in bunks on ship, eating at the crew's mess hall, and purchasing personalized dog tags.

Camden Children's Garden

3 Riverside Dr., Camden; (856) 365-8733; camdenchildrensgarden.org. **Open from April to November, Fri, Sat, Sun, from 10 a.m. to 4 p.m., and in the summer, Thurs, Fri, Sat, Sun, can open other days for group admission; $6 per person,** free **for children 2 and under. $$**

A magical place where nature captures the imagination of children, the Camden Children's Garden features exhibits dedicated to New Jersey's state flower, the violet, and state tree, the red oak; a butterfly house; and the Potting Shed, a make-believe farm where children tend to the farm with wheelbarrows, and then can shop for food and bring it to the kitchen where they can whip up a meal and learn if they've made healthy choices or not.

Camden Riversharks at Campbell's Field

401 N. Delaware Ave.; (856) 963-2600 or (866) SHARKS9; riversharks.com. Visit the website for game schedule. Ticket prices range from $9 to $13 depending on where you choose to sit. $$.

The Camden Riversharks minor league baseball team provides families with affordable entertainment. Take in a game in the state-of-the-art Campbell's Field with its spectacular view of Ben Franklin Bridge and the Philadelphia skyline, which seem as though they are part of the outfield. If the little ones are not satisfied with the game and Cracker Jack alone, they can take a shot on the rock-climbing wall, bouncing inflatables in the fun zone, or the carousel. A 2-hour all-you-can-eat barbecue buffet, from which you can still watch the game, tops the food options at the stadium. Every Friday-night game features a fireworks display in New Jersey's backyard, but right in front of Philly's landmarks.

Susquehanna Bank Center

1 Harbour Blvd., Camden; (856) 365-1300; camdenwaterfront.com/attractions/susquehanna-bank-center. Check website or call ahead for event schedule and ticket prices.

A 25,000-seat outdoor amphitheater, the Susquehanna Bank Center is a great place to take in a show under the stars in the summer. During the winter, the place transforms into a smaller indoor theater. Broadway productions and family-friendly shows are among the programs you might see at the center.

Camden's **Parks**

Camden County is loaded with parks for rest, relaxation, and mostly recreation. Each has its own unique importance worth noting. Here are some of the Camden County parks you might consider visiting:

Berlin Park, between White Horse Pike, Freedom Road, and Park Drive, Berlin; (856) 216-2117. Home to Great Egg Harbor River, this park offers visitors the chance for fishing and hiking lovely nature trails.

Haddon Lake Park, from Station to 10th Avenues, Haddon Heights; (856) 216-2117. Playgrounds are a fun way to pass the time with Haddon Lake in the park.

Hopkins Pond, off Grove Street, on both sides of Hopkins Lane, Haddonfield; (856) 216-2117. A bird sanctuary, a tree trail, and fishing are great attractions for visitors to Hopkins Pond.

Maria Barnaby Greenwald Memorial, Grove Street and Kings Highway, Cherry Hill; (856) 216-2117. You can ride your bike on the trails or take in the wildlife in their natural habitats at this park. A new environmental center is on the horizon.

Newton Lake Park, Cuthbert Boulevard and White Horse Pike; Collingswood, Oaklyn, and Haddon Township; (856) 216-2117. At Newton Lake Park, you can have a picnic, hop on the playground, ride your bike, stroll through the garden, take a boat ride, or go fishing.

Timber Creek Park, Chews Landing Road and Somerdale Road; Lindenwold and Gloucester Township; (856) 216-2117. Timber Creek Park features opportunities for nature trails and even an amphitheater. There are also plans for a children's play area.

For more information, visit camdencounty.com/parks.

Wiggins Park & Marina

Mickle Boulevard at the Delaware River, Camden; (856) 541-7222 or (856) 216-2118; camdenwaterfront.com/attractions/wiggins-park-marina. Check website or call ahead for event schedule and ticket prices.

This is the place to go to see outdoor concerts and shows along the Delaware River with the Philadelphia skyline in the background. Boaters can also dock their vehicles in the marina.

Cooper River Park (all ages)

Bounded by N. and S. Park Drives, Route 130, and Grove Street; (856) 216-2117; camdencounty.com/parks. Open year-round. Admission is free.

Cooper River Park is home to some major rowing competitions, and it runs through Pannsauken, Cherry Hill, Collingswood, and Haddon Township. But there's more to the park than just the river. Bike paths, volleyball courts, softball fields, and a restaurant, **The Lobster Trap,** provide visitors with an ample list of things to do. There's no chance of getting bored at this park. If those other activities don't do it for you, you can always battle each other on the mini golf course, walk through the sculpture garden, or frolic on the playground.

Harleigh Cemetery (ages 6 and up)

1640 Haddon Ave., Collingswood/Camden; (856) 963-3500; harleighcemetery.org. Open Mon through Sat from 8:30 a.m. to 4:30 p.m. Free.

Walt Whitman lived in Camden, and he died in Camden. And he's still in Camden. While it might seem ghoulish to bring children to a cemetery, this is the final resting place of one of the country's best-loved poets. You could share Whitman's poems with your children as a segue to the visit. The tomb in which Whitman's remains lie was actually designed by the poet himself. And historic Harleigh Cemetery, which dates back to 1885, is well manicured and features a section for veterans as well.

Pennypacker Park (all ages)

Park Boulevard and Grove Street, Haddonfield; (856) 216-2117; camdencounty .com/parks/parks/pennypacker-park. Open year-round. Admission is free.

Pennypacker Park is the perfect spot if your kid is yearning to be a paleontologist. A stone and plaque commemorate the site where in 1858 William Foulke unearthed the first nearly complete dinosaur skeleton. Visiting this park is a great excuse to talk dinosaur with the kids. You could serve them up an interesting lesson about fossils and prehistoric times. Dinosaur lovers call this the ground zero of paleontology, and visitors can still climb down toward the ravine where the remains were found.

The Walt Whitman House (ages 6 and up)
330 Mickle Blvd., Camden; (856) 964-5383; state.nj.us/dep/parksandforests. Call ahead to confirm hours of operation and tour availability; open Wed through Sat from 10 a.m. to noon and 1 to 4 p.m., and on Sun from 1 to 4 p.m.; closed Mon, Tues, most state and federal holidays, and Wed following a state or federal holiday. Admission is free.

Walt Whitman first lived in Camden with his brother George. When George and his wife moved to Burlington, Whitman chose to stay in Camden. Thanks to his successful *Leaves of Grass,* he bought his own home for $1,750. "Camden was originally an accident, but I shall never be sorry I was left over in Camden," Whitman wrote, according to The Walt Whitman House website. "It has brought me blessed returns." He invited a friend Mary O. Davis to live with him and serve as his housekeeper, and the two lived there together until his death in 1892. While he lived in Camden, contemporary artists visited him, including Thomas Eakins, Bram Stoker, and Oscar Wilde. Upon visiting The Walt Whitman House, you'll be greeted by the poet's letters, photographs from the 19th century, the bed in which Whitman died, and the death notice that was nailed to the door. You might also plan your trip around certain events, such as the annual celebration of Whitman's birthday in May, which includes the winners of a high school poetry contest held in the poet's honor.

Where to Eat

Caffe Aldo Lamberti. 2011 Rte. 70 West, Cherry Hill; (856) 663-1747; caffelamberti .com. Open Mon through Thurs from 11:30 a.m. to 10 p.m., Fri from 11:30 a.m. to 11 p.m., Sat from noon to 11 p.m., and Sun from 1 to 9 p.m. (dinner only). Despite the average dinner costing $40, this is a family-friendly place with lots of charm. $$$$

Sammy Chon's K Town BBQ. 404 Marlton Pike East (Route 70), Sawmill Village, Cherry Hill; (856) 216-0090; ktownbbq.com. Open 7 days a week from 11 a.m. to 10 p.m. From seafood to meat, this restaurant promises to deliver Korean barbecue at its best. $$

Where to Stay

Days Inn & Suites Cherry Hill–Philadelphia. 525 Rte. 38 East; (856) 663-0100; daysinn.com. A well-manicured landscape and 86 recently renovated rooms are the highlights of this hotel. $

Holiday Inn Philadelphia–Cherry Hill. 2175 Marlton Pike Rd. West, Cherry Hill; (856) 663-5300; holidayinn.com. Conveniently located, this hotel is great for families on road trips who want to see both New Jersey and Philly. $$

Gloucester County

A mecca for farming, Gloucester County is famous for its homegrown agriculture. With a flourishing dairy industry, the county is also well known for its breeding of cattle, hogs, and other livestock. To support those industries, there are canneries, quick-freezing establishments, and markets that thrive. Although farming is the name of the game in Gloucester County, many of the nearly 288,300 residents take advantage of its proximity to Philadelphia. Like the rest of New Jersey, Gloucester County boasts numerous connections to the Revolutionary War and colonial times.

Bellmawr Lake (all ages)

850 Creek Rd., Bellmawr; (856) 933-0554; bellmawrlake.net. Open 7 days a week in the summer (Mon through Sat: swimming from 10 a.m. to 6 p.m., picnic grounds from 10 a.m. to 7 p.m., beach bar from 11:30 a.m. to 6 p.m.; Sun and holidays: swimming from 9:30 a.m. to 6 p.m., picnic grounds from 9:30 a.m. to 7 p.m., beach bar from 11 a.m. to 6 p.m.). General admission on weekdays costs $8 for adults and $6 for children ages 2 to 11; general admission for weekends and holidays costs $10 for adults ages 12 and over and $7 for children ages 2 to 11. **Free** for children under 2. A $1 entrance card fee for each guest on his or her first visit.

In addition to being a great site for family reunions and other parties, Bellmawr Lake offers visitors the chance to swim, picnic, play volleyball, partake in minigolf, or lounge by the bar. There is even a 100-foot water slide. And horseshoes is the perfect game for old-fashioned fun with the family.

New Jersey **Goes Hollywood**

In recent years, New Jersey has become a popular setting for television and film. While some of these titles are not appropriate for the kids, parents might get a kick out of viewing them ahead of a trip through the Garden State. You can always choose one of the family-friendly options for your next movie night. Here is a list of the more popular TV series and movies in which New Jersey is a star:

Television
Boardwalk Empire—Visit the underworld in Atlantic City back in the day.

The Sopranos—Visit the underworld in northern New Jersey in contemporary times.

Run's House—Join Reverend Run and his family as they deal with life and fame from their New Jersey home.

Cake Boss—Discover the joys of running a family bakery in Hoboken.

Real Housewives of New Jersey—Learn about how not to act at dinner parties and virtually anyplace else from these Jersey girls with bad manners.

Jersey Shore—Although many of the seasons of this reality show take place on the Jersey Shore, most of the badly behaving cast are not true Jerseyans.

Jerseylicious—Admire the big hair and big attitudes of the Jersey girls (and guys) working at a typical hair salon.

Jersey Couture—Feel as though you are a part of this family as it runs a dress shop in the Garden State.

Movies
Dogma—When good versus evil comes to Jersey, everyone gets in on the fight.

Garden State—A troubled young man returns to the suburbs and makes you feel more normal.

Mallrats—Get an insider's look at the subculture of most Jersey young adults, who spend half their lives at the mall.

The Crossing—Receive an education in history by witnessing George Washington's heroics while in New Jersey during the Revolutionary War.

Paul Blart: Mall Cop—Get a load of how this "cop" saves the mall and Black Friday from scheming thieves.

The Wedding Singer—Feel like the BFF to Adam Sandler and Drew Barrymore as they fall in love to the tunes of the 1980s in Ridgefield, NJ.

Cheaper by the Dozen—Get a few laughs and a few lessons from this large family trying to make it through the good and the bad in Jersey.

Date Night—Join this typical couple from northern New Jersey as they try to avoid very bad cops who are trying to kill them while on their date night in nearby NYC.

Big—Become a kid again yourself while you watch Tom Hanks going from child to adult overnight.

Confessions of a Teenage Drama Queen—Find out what happens when a teenage girl moves to the Jersey suburbs with her family.

Jersey Girl—Although this flick was a flop, you get to see Ben Affleck in action as a single dad. Isn't that enough?

Miss Congeniality—Sandra Bullock shines as a tomboy FBI agent posing as a girly-girl pageant contestant to save the competition from what could be a fatal explosion.

Candor Hall or Ladd's Castle (all ages)

1337 LaFayette Ave., Colonial Manor, West Deptford; co.gloucester.nj.us. You can see the building year-round for free.

A trip to West Deptford is the chance to see the country's oldest brick house, Candor Hall or Ladd's Castle, which was built around 1688 by John Ladd. Aside from the home's importance for its age, it has historical significance because Ladd reportedly helped William Penn plan Philadelphia.

Creamy Acres Farm (all ages)

448 Lincoln Mill Rd., Mullica Hill; (856) 223-1669; creamyacres.com. Open spring through fall. Prices vary depending on events you attend or if you shop on the premises.

The kids will adore the barn at Creamy Acres Farm, where they can get acquainted with baby animals—calves, bunnies, chicks, and more. And you'll enjoy the store, where you can pick up Jersey Fresh produce and specialty salsa and jams. You can also pick up plants and other treasures at the garden center. Even if it's raining, you can check out the greenhouse. If boredom sets in for the kids, there's always the playground on-site to keep them busy. You can also take a dairy tour or participate in the special events that take place in the fall, including wagon rides and a cornfield maze for younger kids and the Night of Terror for older ones who don't mind a bit of fright.

Edelman Planetarium at Rowan University (all ages)

Science Hall, Rowan University, 201 Mullica Hill Rd., Glassboro; (856) 256-4389; rowan.edu/planetarium. Check website for shows and schedule. Admission costs $5 for adults, $3 for children, seniors, and Rowan students.

Consider the cosmos at Rowan University's Edelman Planetarium, where you can get educated while taking in a show about the universe. The planetarium has featured laser shows and public star shows. Every year in December, the planetarium is the place to be for the *Season of Light* show, which has spectators learning about winter and how people brought light to the darkest time of the year. The planetarium is a great way to introduce your kids to stargazing and the universe beyond the world we know.

Heritage Glass Museum (ages 6 and up)

25 E. High St., Glassboro; (856) 881-7468; heritageglassmuseum.com. Open Sat from 11 a.m. to 2 p.m., Wed from noon to 3 p.m., and the fourth Sun of the month from 1 to 4 p.m.; closed Wed in July and Aug. Admission is **free,** but donations are encouraged.

Filled with fragile glass vessels, dishes, bowls, vases, and bottles, the Heritage Glass Museum is an homage to South Jersey's glass-making tradition. Highlights include a 1784 Heston Bottle, antique glassmaker's tools, and South Jersey paperweights. Demijohns, fruit jars, and glass company money are among the museum's other treasures. There are also changing displays that feature exhibits that are special to the museum. A recent example was South Jersey glass from the book of Thomas Haunton, a South Jersey glass historian, author, and collector. Just be sure your kids are mature enough to walk the museum without trying to grab or break glass.

Red Bank Battlefield Park (all ages)

100 Hessian Ave., National Park; (856) 853-5120; co.gloucester.nj.us. Open Apr to mid-October for tours Wed through Sun from 1 to 4 p.m.; there are also special events during other parts of the year; check the website for details. Admission is **free.**

Red Bank Battlefield Park is home to lots of history. The most noteworthy element of the park is the **James & Ann Whitall House,** which was built in 1748 and remained the home of the Whitall family for 114 years. The home, which exhibits the Georgian style, played a pivotal role in the American Revolution. Close to Fort Mercer, which is where the Battle of Red Bank was fought and won by the American troops, the home served as a hospital for the wounded. Mrs. Whitall was among those who nursed them. After that, the entire Whitall family returned and tended to the surrounding plantation and created numerous businesses, including a mill and smokehouse. For four generations, the family lived and worked there. Today, visitors are welcome to tour the home and partake in special events, such as the Herb Garden Flower Show, Colonial Christmas, and Children's History Encampment.

On the same battlefield, you can visit the remnants of **Fort Mercer,** which was built by the Americans during the Revolution and, along with Fort Mifflin, was meant to protect the Philadelphia Harbor and communities on the Delaware River. It was destroyed after the Americans won the Battle of Red Bank. Besides the James and Ann Whitall House and Fort Mercer, visitors to the Red Bank Battlefield Park can picnic, jog, walk, or enjoy the playground.

Where to Eat

Landmark Americana Tap & Grill. 1 Mullica Hill Rd., Glassboro; (856) 863-6600; landmarkamericana.com. Pub pizzas and buffalo wings will hit the sweet spot when you're craving bar food, and they should also satisfy the kids. Open for lunch and dinner. $–$$

Nick's Pizza. 644 Delsea Dr., Glassboro; (856) 307-1100; nickspizzaonline.com. Open every day at 11 a.m. Simple offerings of pizza, stromboli, and calzone are sure to please little ones and adults alike. $

Terra Nova. 590 Delsea Dr., Sewell; (856) 589-8883; terranovawineanddine.com. Open every day for lunch and dinner. Sushi and seafood are among your top choices at this restaurant. $$

Where to Stay

Fairfield Inn Deptford. 1160 Hurffville Rd., Deptford; (856) 686-9050; marriott .com. Close to the Liberty Bell, Fairfield Inn guests are not limited only to Jersey attractions. $$

Salem County

With little more than 66,000 people, Salem County has the smallest population of any New Jersey county. What it lacks in residents, it more than makes up for in natural beauty. It boasts six rivers, meadow and marshland, tidal and freshwater wetlands, 40 lakes and ponds, dunes, and more. In fact, half the county's land is dedicated to farms. Visitors can take advantage of the country feel of the county—and the opportunities for one-on-one interaction with wildlife, agriculture, and plant life. This is one part of New Jersey that has small town appeal, which families can appreciate.

Camp Crockett County Park (all ages)

Avis Mill Road, Pilesgrove; (856) 935-7510 ext 8223; njwildlifetrails.org. Open from mid-April through the end of Oct from 8 a.m. to dusk; call ahead to have access to the gate from November 1 to mid-April when no one is on-site; weekend visitors all year must also call ahead. Free.

Camp Crockett County Park offers the chance for encounters with wildlife through all four seasons. You can meet red fox, white-tailed deer, and wild turkey in winter; herons and egrets in the spring; snakes and turtles in the summer; and migrating ducks and foraging squirrels in the fall. If seeking out wildlife bores your little ones, you can head to the playground or picnic area. Canoeing and kayaking are fun family activities that allow you to get up close and personal with some of the wildlife. And if you visit in the spring, you'll be treated to beautiful flowering trees and wildflowers.

Cowtown Rodeo (all ages)

780 Harding Hwy., Pilesgrove; (856) 769-3200; cowtownrodeo.com. Gates open every Sat night at 6 p.m. for 7:30 p.m. show. Tickets cost $15 for adults, $10 for children ages 12 and under, and free for children under 2.

The east coast of New Jersey, which has a rep for being the land of the Guido and the gateway to Philadelphia and New York, has another side to it. This other side is where one meets the Garden State's country flair. The best place to do this is at Cowtown Rodeo, a weekly rodeo since 1957. If you turn out for one of the Saturday shows, you'll take in bull riding, bareback bronc riding, and girls' barrel racing, just to name a few. There's also a flea market if you feel like shopping.

Giant Pumpkin Carve (all ages)

Salem County Fair Grounds, Route 40, Pilesgrove; giantpumpkincarve.com. Happens on the third Sat in Oct every year. Proceeds from admission go to charity.

Since 1996, the people of Salem County have enjoyed the Giant Pumpkin Carve, an annual event that has local artists showing off their pumpkin-carving skills. In addition to checking out the pumpkins, you can participate in free hay rides, a straw maze, and the crowning of the Pumpkin Princess. Kids can dress up in costume, and you can all enjoy the musical entertainment.

Hancock House (ages 6 and up)

3 Front St., Hancocks Bridge; (856) 935-4373; nj.gov/dep/parksandforests. Open Wed through Sat from 10 a.m. to noon and 1 to 4 p.m., and Sun from 1 to 4 p.m.; closed Mon, Tues, most state and federal holidays, and Wed following state and federal holidays. Admission is free for all.

The Hancock House holds a special place in American history. In March 1778, on the orders of Gen. Charles Mawhood, the British stormed the Hancock House and bayoneted the members of the Continental Army stationed inside. Judge William Hancock, a member of the family who owned the home, was among the victims. Judge Hancock's great-uncle, English shoemaker William Hancock, bought the property from John Fenwick in 1675. Eventually, William's nephew John inherited the property and helped develop the community. John's son William and his wife Sarah built the Hancock House in 1734. Their son William, who succeeded his father as a judge, was the one who was killed in the massacre.

Still, the Hancocks remained in the house until 1931. But some believe the house was used as a tavern in the 18th and 19th century. Today it is a museum. While the historical significance of the home is important to note, so is the architecture, which represents an example of typical Quaker construction with patterned brickwork. You might plan your trip to Hancock House around its many events, which have included a children's workshop on colonial games and crafts, a spring tea, a crab and craft festival, and an ice-cream social.

Family Farm **Fun**

Salem County is mostly farmland, which means the place is oozing with charm and family-friendly activities. Here are the farms that you can visit for a bit of country fun, including corn mazes, hayrides, pumpkin picking, and cut-your-own Christmas trees:

Coombs' Barnyard, 20 Rte. 77, Elmer; (856) 358-5169; coombsbarn yard.com. Stock up on potatoes or pumpkins (depending on the time of year you visit), enjoy hayrides, barrel train rides, and petting the barn animals, including hogs. And learn about life on the farm from the ninth generation of Coombs to run the place.

Scarecrow Hollow Cornfield Maze, 335 Quinton Hancock's Bridge Rd., Salem; (856) 935-3469; scarecrowhollow.org. At different events throughout the year, you can build a scarecrow, find your way through the inventive corn mazes, and have the kids' faces painted.

Stimpson's Tree Farm, 245 Friendship Rd., Monroeville; (856) 358-2384; stimpsonstreefarm.com. Anyone who wants to cut down their own Christmas tree or would like to walk through an 80-acre field smelling pine—and feeling the Christmas spirit—won't want to miss Stimpson's.

Nanticoke Lenni-Lenape Annual Pow Wow (all ages)

Salem County Fair Grounds, Route 40, Pilesgrove; (856) 769-3200; nanticoke-lenape.info/powwow.htm. Happens annually in the summer. Admission is free for all.

New Jersey's original residents, the Lenni Lenape Native Americans, still share their culture every year at the Nanticoke Lenni-Lenape Annual Pow Wow. You can visit the grounds and watch the Lenni Lenape dance or observe their worship service. It's a chance to have the kids get a firsthand look at the first people to live in New Jersey and call it home.

Parvin State Park (all ages)

701 Almond Rd., Pittsgrove; (856) 358-8616; state.nj.us/dep/parksandforests. Open daily sunrise to sunset; office is open Mon through Fri from 8 a.m. to 4 p.m. Entrance fees, which vary, are charged from Memorial Day through Labor Day; children under 3 are free.

On the edge of the Pine Barrens, Parvin State Park features New Jersey's favorite pines but also a swamp hardwood forest. You can camp on the grounds or take a swim in Parvin Lake, which is staffed with a lifeguard. Along with Thundergust Lake and Muddy Run, Parvin Lake is popular for fishing. Picnic areas, replete with grills, offer a pleasant place to chill with the family. There are trails for hiking. And you might find the threatened barred owl and endangered swamp pink. The state recommends visiting in the spring when everything is blooming—from magnolia to dogwood.

Supawna Meadows National Wildlife Refuge (all ages)

197 Lighthouse Rd., Pennsville; (609) 463-0994; fws.gov/supawnameadows. Open year-round. Free.

Part of the Cape May National Wildlife Refuge, the Supawna Meadows National Wildlife Refuge encompasses 3,000 acres and plays an important role in the fall and spring migration of many waterfowl. A visit is the chance to see black ducks, mallards, and northern pintails in the winter and sandpipers and shorebirds in the summer. While migrating, warblers, sparrows, and others use the site as a resting and feeding area. Junior birders might also spot osprey, bald eagles, and owls.

Where to Eat

Helen's Cafe & Gardens. 450 Telegraph Rd., Alloway; (856) 935-4380; helenscafe
andgardens.com. Open Wed through Fri from 6 a.m. to 2:30 p.m., Sat and Sun from
6 a.m. to noon. Closed Mon and Tues. Here, you will find affordable lunch items—
including soup in a bread boule or hot sandwiches, such as a pizza cheesesteak. Private tea parties and children's birthdays are also possibilities. $

Salem City Cafe, 113–119 Market St., Salem; (856) 339-4455; salemcitycafe.com.
Open for lunch Tues through Fri from 11:30 a.m. to 3 p.m. and for dinner Wed through
Sat from 5 to 10 p.m. Closed Sun and Mon. Almond-crusted tilapia and vodka cream
sauce over linguine or penne are among your menu options. $$

Where to Stay

Hampton Inn Pennsville. 429 N. Broadway, Pennsville; (856) 351-1700; hampton
inn1.hilton.com. This is another hotel that is great for those on a road trip because it's
close to Wilmington, Philadelphia, Atlantic City, and Washington, DC. $$

Holiday Inn Express. 506 Pennsville Auburn Rd., Carneys Point; (856) 351-9222;
hiexpress.com. Holiday Inn Express hotels have a reputation for providing guests with
clean, comfortable accommodations at affordable prices. $$

Cumberland County

Once famous for its oysters (Port Norris was once known as the "Oyster Capital of the World") and glass, Cumberland County now earns a living through health care, construction, hospitality/tourism, and manufacturing industries. Breaking away from Salem County in 1748, Cumberland County remains small with a population of a little more than 156,000 and 14 communities. Agriculture remains a big part of the Cumberland County lifestyle. As a result, visitors can enjoy the nature that is all around them.

Cumberland Players at the Little Theatre

Sherman Avenue and the Boulevard, Vineland; (856) 692-5626; cumberlandplayers .com. Check website for shows and times. Prices depend on the show you wish to attend and your seat.

Launched in 1946, the Cumberland Players at the Little Theatre put on about 3 shows per season. The cast and crew continue to be made up entirely of volunteers who love the stage. In the summer, you can catch the annual musical, which has included *Fiddler on the Roof, My Fair Lady, the King and I,* and *Camelot. Little Shop of Horrors, The Diary of Anne Frank,* and *It's a Wonderful Life: A Live Radio Play* are among the other plays that have been performed. Check the website for a schedule.

Maurice River

Vineland, Buena Vista Township, Millville, Maurice River Township, and Commercial Township; mauriceriver.igc.org. Open year-round. Free.

Four of the five towns through which the Maurice River and its tributaries (Menantico, Manumuskin, and Muskee) run are in Cumberland County. This was the source of all those oysters. Birding is a popular pastime here. There are large populations of bald eagles around the Maurice River. You can also check out the typical Pinelands plant life around the river and its tributaries. The Manumuskin River is home to 32 rare plants, including the sensitive joint vetch, for which there are only five strands known worldwide. And 15 of the state's 25 threatened and endangered bird species breed at the Manumuskin.

While in the area, you can also learn about the community's past. In Millville, Wheaton Village features the **Museum of American Glass,** a re-created 1888 glass factory, and a stained glass studio. There are daily demonstrations of glassmaking, pottery, and woodworking. In Commercial Township, you can hop aboard a floating museum, the *A. J. Meerwald,* a restored 1928 oyster schooner, and stop by the nearby maritime museum in Port Norris. If you visit in June, you can attend Delaware Bay Day, which includes Jersey Fresh seafood, musical entertainment, and children's games.

The Off Broad Street Players

Bridgeton and Millville; (845) 451-5437; obsp.org. Check website for shows and times. Call or visit the website for prices and ticket sales.
A regional community theater, The Off Broad Street Players (OBSP) put on shows at the Trinity United Methodist Church in Bridgeton, Bridgeton High School, or the Glassworks in Millville. Having grown from 10 participants in 1998, when the theater troupe launched, to 100-plus members today, the OBSP has performed *Annie, The Sound of Music, Brighton Beach Memoirs,* and *Nunsense.* You can check the website or call for show dates and to purchase tickets.

Riverfront Renaissance Center for the Arts

22 N. High St., Millville; (856) 327-4500; rrcarts.com. Open Sun through Thurs from 11 a.m. to 5 p.m., Fri from 11 a.m. to 6 p.m., third Fri of the month 11 a.m. to 9 p.m., and Sat from 11 a.m. to 6 p.m. You can become a member to support the center.
An art gallery that changes its exhibits every third Friday of the month, the Riverfront Renaissance Center for the Arts offers visitors the chance to appreciate glass, photographs, student artwork, and more. There are 4 galleries, each with its own unique style and each with the same mission: to serve as a backdrop for

The **Byways**

New Jersey's byways are wonderful places to admire nature and see the softer side of the state. A car ride through each is worth your time if you seek visions of wildlife, plants, and a bit of history and adventure.

Delaware River Scenic Byway

The nearly 33-mile Delaware River Scenic Byway runs from Trenton, New Jersey's capital, to Frenchtown. Along the way, you can get up close with history in the towns that once played a pivotal role in the birth of the nation. You can also enjoy the Delaware and Raritan Canal (D&R Canal), which provided power during the Industrial Revolution and today is a source of entertainment and water supply. In the spring, you might want to check out the living history programs along the way.

Millstone Valley Scenic Byway

The D&R Canal makes an appearance in the nearly 28-mile Millstone Valley Scenic Byway, too. You might consider bicycling the D&R Canal Towpath in these parts. A ride through this byway gives visitors a sense of the canal era and early American and Dutch heritage, not to mention additional sites related to the American Revolution.

Bayshore Heritage Byway

The 122-mile Bayshore Heritage Byway is located in Salem, Cumberland, and Cape May Counties along the Delaware River and Delaware Bayshore. It features historical sites and lots of wildlife, so keep your eyes peeled.

Palisades Scenic Byway

Resting upon the 500-foot tall Palisades Cliffs, the Palisades Scenic Byway offers incredible views of the George Washington Bridge and Manhattan skyline. In fact, you can enter the bridge in Fort Lee, the gateway to New York City, on one end of the 19-mile byway and ride up through cozy hamlets in New York State on the other.

Pine Barrens Byway

This 130-mile byway is home to the 1.1-million–acre Pinelands, the largest forested space in the Mid-Atlantic region. An estuary and marshes are among the highlights. Nature lovers will enjoy passing through this area for the wildlife and plants. It is the Pine Barrens that keep New Jersey honest; without them—and their cranberry and blueberry industries—the state would have little reason to keep its moniker as the Garden State.

Upper Freehold Historic Farmland Byway

On the 24-mile path you can visit Allentown, a colonial town that remains virtually untouched. It's also a great place to see agricultural activity in action.

Warren Heritage Scenic Byway

Otherwise known as Route 57, the 21-mile Warren Heritage Scenic Byway runs from Hackettstown to Lopatcong and sits atop old Native American trails.

For more information about New Jersey's byways, visit byways.org/explore/states/NJ.

artwork that should be the center of attention. Children ages 7 and up are eligible for some of the art classes that are offered at Riverfront Renaissance Center for the Arts.

Where to Eat

Cosmopolitan: Restaurant, Lounge, Bakery. 3513 S. Delsea Dr., Vineland; (856) 765-5977; cosmopolitannj.com. Serving everything from barbecue to pasta, Cosmopolitan offers something for everyone, and the diverse price range helps families stick to their own budget. $–$$$

Esposito's Maplewood III. 200 N. Delsea Dr., Vineland; (856) 692-2011; maplewood3.com. Open Mon through Sat for dinner and Sun for lunch and dinner. Italian seafood dishes at decent prices are the draw at this restaurant, which has been in business since 1983. $$$

Winfields Restaurant. 106 N. High St., Millville; (856) 327-0909; winfieldsrestaurant.com. Open Tues through Sun for dinner. Catering to a sophisticated palette, this restaurant serves dishes, such as rack of lamb and risotto. $$$

Where to Stay

Fairfield Inn & Suites Millville Vineland. 301 Bluebird Ln., Millville; (856) 776-2400; marriott.com. The colorful lobby and bed linens are so cheery that you can't help but have fun. $–$$

Holiday Inn Express Vineland Millville. 398 Smith St., Vineland; (856) 293-8888; hiexpress.com. A warm lobby and 100 guest rooms make this hotel inviting. $$

Quality Inn & Suites. 1701 S. 2nd St., Millville; (856) 327-3300; qualityinn.com. Close to the Maurice River and Glasstown Arts District, this hotel is conveniently located and quite affordable. $

The Ramada Vineland. 2216 W. Landis Ave., Vineland; (856) 696-3800; ramada vineland.com. Recently renovated, the Ramada Vineland boasts new bedding and **free** continental breakfast with hot items. Kids 17 and under stay **free** with an adult. $$

Wingate by Wyndham Vineland, 2196 W. Landis Ave., Vineland; (856) 690-9900; wingatehotels.com. Close to all the hot spots, this bargain hotel offers the usual amenities, including *USA Today* at your room's door. $

Atlantic County

Once famous for its shipbuilding industry, Atlantic County is now most famous for its casinos in Atlantic City. While casinos aren't exactly family-friendly places, the Boardwalk and surrounding neighborhoods offer something for the kids, too. It wasn't always that way. In the late 1800s, Atlantic City took off as a tourism destination and truly hit its stride with adults in the 1920s, only to lose its appeal when air travel became more commonplace and people were jetting to warmer climates in the 1950s. Although the city faced decline for many years, the arrival of the casinos in the late 1970s started to turn things around. AC gained a reputation for its nightlife and adult pursuits. But in the last decade, the county as a whole has tried to come up with more options for families. Lucky for you, there are now plenty of things for kids to do, not just in Atlantic City but across the county. And there's history to boot with attractions, such as Lucy the Elephant in Margate and the Absecon Lighthouse, the tallest lighthouse in New Jersey, which has been restored to its former glory.

The Atlantic City Boardwalk

Boardwalk Information Center, 2301 Boardwalk, Boardwalk Hall, Atlantic City; (888) AC-VISIT; atlanticcitynj.com. Open year-round, but some attractions are closed in the winter. Strolling down the Boardwalk is free, but its attractions, stores, and eateries vary in cost.

The longest boardwalk in the world, the one in Atlantic City is appropriately referred to simply as "The Boardwalk." There are many lovely distractions as you walk along The Boardwalk. One of them is the **New Jersey Korean War Memorial,** which features sculptures of soldiers standing tall; it honors those who served and helped bring democracy to South Korea. Dollar stores, casinos aglow in lights, and reminders of the city's glory days might also catch your eye. The Boardwalk is the heart of the county's tourism, and its offshoot piers offer many attractions and activities for travelers.

Of all the piers, the most famous has to be the **Steel Pier,** whose origins date back to 1898. In its heyday, it attracted thousands of visitors and would reach a peak of about 80,000 on the Sunday before Labor Day, according to its website. When Atlantic City's resorts decayed in the 1960s and 1970s, so did the Steel Pier. In 1982, it was wiped out by fire. But in 1993, thanks to Donald Trump's Taj Mahal resort, the Steel Pier was revived. Today, there are 24 rides, games and prizes, a food court, and **free** admission at the Steel Pier. One of the highlights for kids is the double-decker carousel designed by Italian crafts-men and featuring scenes from Atlantic City's illustrious history. Families can always hop aboard the iconic Ferris wheel, which invites guests from the other parts of the Boardwalk with its brilliant lights and STEEL PIER sign. Thrill seekers can take a spin on the Rocket, which bills itself as "225 feet of pure adrenalin."

To continue the fun, you can head to the **Central Pier Arcade & Speedway** at 1400 Boardwalk. Here, you can experience one of the largest over and under racetracks with NASCAR-style go-karts. Challenge your family members to a paintball tournament. Or take your chances with the games, such as cranes, slot machines, and skeeball, for which you can collect points for prizes that include everything from plush animals to laptop computers.

When you tire of playing, you can lounge on the beach, which is right off the Boardwalk and makes for a refreshing retreat on a hot summer's day. The kids can play in the sand or take a dip in the ocean, while you work on your tan Jersey style. For another Jerseyesque escapade, you and the family can stop by the mall. The Boardwalk is now home to the **Pier Shops at Caesars,** a high-end shopping center. IT'SUGAR is a rainbow-colored den of sweets that will have the kids on a sugar high. And if you hit the jackpot, you can pick up diamonds at Tif-fany & Co. Even if you're not game for purchasing anything, you can take a stroll and do some window-shopping. There is also an area, replete with sand and lounge chairs, that has you taking in views of the beach and heat from the sun from behind large glass windows, which is particularly welcoming come winter. Children often play in that sand as though they were actually on the beach. And you can't miss the fountain show, which happens at regular intervals throughout the day and has dancing water delightfully set to the beat of music and lights that change color.

If you want to do some actual shopping and the Pier Shops are simply not your style (or in your budget), you can walk a bit off the Boardwalk to **The Walk,** which are relatively new outlet stores. Among the shops are Tommy Hilfiger, Banana Republic, Aeropostale, and more. Whatever you do, don't leave The Boardwalk without picking up saltwater taffy or fudge, two of the city's specialties.

Atlantic City Boardwalk Hall (all ages)

2301 Boardwalk, Atlantic City; (609) 348-7000; boardwalkhall.com. Open year-round. Check website for shows, times, and tickets.
Formerly the Atlantic City Convention Center, Boardwalk Hall is the center of the Boardwalk and the center of entertainment. For more than 80 years, the hall has hosted everything from epic boxing matches to thrilling live concerts. It is the site of the first indoor college football game and first indoor helicopter ride. The Army Air Forces used the hall as a training center during World War II. And everyone from Frank Sinatra to the Rolling Stones has performed there. Today you can visit the renovated and newly named hall to see all kinds of performances and events. Indoor auto racing, concerts, and a rodeo are among recent shows.

Atlantic City Historical Museum (ages 6 and up)

Boardwalk, Garden Pier, Atlantic City; (609) 347-5839; acmuseum.org. Open daily from 10 a.m. to 4 p.m. Admission is free for all.
On the Boardwalk's Garden Pier, you'll find the Atlantic City Historical Museum, which features the **Al Gold Photography Gallery,** which is named for famous photographer Al Gold. He photographed the first Miss America pageant and became AC's chief photographer. In his gallery, you can see rotating photography exhibits that speak to the city's unique history. The permanent exhibit space includes Miss America memorabilia, a miniature beach and sand-art exhibit, and Mr. Peanut, who greets visitors as they enter. You can also visit the nearby Atlantic City Art Center.

Haunted Tales (all ages)

1535 Boardwalk, Atlantic City; (609) 340-8818; atlanticcitynj.com. Open daily year-round, from noon to 6 p.m. in winter, and from noon to 1 a.m. in summer. $7.50 for adults, $6.50 for kids 12 and under. $$.

A 4-D theatrical experience, *Haunted Tales* has audience members listening to the tales of the Jersey Devil and New Jersey pirates who haunt the Jersey Shore. At the same time, the interactive theater has all sorts of other special effects to pump up the fear factor. While some kids will find this amusing and fun, others will be scared. Know your kid and decide accordingly whether this is an appropriate activity.

Ripley's Believe It or Not Museum (all ages)

1441 Boardwalk, Atlantic City; (609) 347-2001; ripleys.com/atlanticcity. Open year-round but hours vary by season, so check the website. Admission costs $15.99 for adults ages 13 and up, $9.99 for children ages 5 to 12, and free for children 4 and younger. The Vault Laser race costs $3 for one play and $5 for two plays. If your kids are into all things weird, then they'll love Ripley's. In the Odditorium, you can observe the stomach contents of a 17-year-old girl who griped about a bellyache, a shrunken head, the world's smallest production car, a roulette table made of 14,000 jelly beans, and optical illusions galore. The laser maze challenges visitors to get through a room filled with green laser lights without breaking any of the beams and as quickly as they can. Play against yourself or

Atlantic City **Tours**

Through **Atlantic City Tours,** you can book trolley and boat tours of Atlantic City and nearby sites, such as Philadelphia's waterfront and Cape May. Examples of the AC-centric tours you might book include the Splash of Atlantic City Trolley Tour, which includes stops at historic Absecon Lighthouse and the Atlantic City Aquarium, a Harbor Cruise in Atlantic City that brings guests to the harbors and marinas of Brigantine Beach and historic Gardner's Basin, or a shopping tour with stops at The Walk outlets. Dolphin-watching cruises and one on shipwrecks in the area are among the other highlights perfect for families.

There are various departure points, depending on the tour you book; (800) 208-4421; atlanticcitytours.net. Check website for availability of tours, times, and prices.

play against your family. Every year, contestants compete in the Great Face Off to determine who has the weirdest face in Atlantic City. You can throw your hat—err, face—in the ring.

African American Heritage Museum (all ages)

661 Jackson Rd., Newtonville; (609) 704-5495; aahmsnj.org. Open Tues through Sat from 10 a.m. to 4 p.m. Closed Sun and Mon. Admission is free for all.

At the African American Heritage Museum, you can investigate the history of the African-American experience in the 20th century. Exhibits feature photos, graphics, and even items from popular culture (such as Wheaties boxes) to showcase the cultural evolution African Americans have undergone. A decade-by-decade look that takes visitors from Aunt Jemima to Tiger Woods offers insight into the struggles for equality and the accomplishments and contributions African Americans have made to the world. Rotating exhibits have included one on the history of coiled basket making in Africa and the US.

Historic Gardner's Basin (all ages)

800 N. New Hampshire Ave., Atlantic City; (609) 348-2880; atlanticcitynj.com. Open year-round but seasonal attractions are closed for the winter. Prices vary depending on the activities you choose to experience.

Once the home of commercial fishing fleets and rumrunners, Historic Gardner's Basin now welcomes visitors who come for deep-sea and back-bay fishing or for cruises that leave from there. A colony of artists who work their magic at the basin, restaurants, and the Diving Bell, which used to be at the Steel Pier, draw guests for the day. But the most popular attraction at the basin is the Atlantic City Aquarium, which deserves its own listing (see below) because it's an educational and fun locale for families.

Atlantic City Aquarium (all ages)

800 N. New Hampshire Ave., Atlantic City; (609) 348-2880; oceanlifecenter .com. Open daily from 10 a.m. to 5 p.m. Admission costs $8 for adults, $6 for seniors ages 62 and up, $5 for children ages 4 to 12, free for children under 3.

The Atlantic City Aquarium brings creatures of the sea to the public—and it offers an education about them to boot. Some of the most popular exhibits include the feedings by divers, live coral, loggerhead sea turtles, and ocean oddities. The Mullica River tank features sea life that is typical of the local cedar-water tributaries of the Pine Barrens.

Civil Rights Garden (all ages)

Pacific Avenue and Dr. Martin Luther King Boulevard, Atlantic City; (609) 347-0500. Open year-round. Free to walk through the park.
Featuring 11 granite sculptures, the Civil Rights Garden is an artistic homage to the figures that played a role in the civil rights movement. The winding pathways, plants, and flowers, make for a tranquil setting in which to teach the kids about those who had the courage to fight for what they believed and seek true equality for all.

Historic Smithville & Village Greene (all ages)

1 N. New York Rd., Smithville; (609) 748-6160; smithvillenj.com/index.cfm or historic smithvillenj.com. Open year-round. Prices vary, depending on which shops and eateries you frequent.
Historic Smithville & Village Greene, with their cobblestone paths and old-fashioned taverns, takes visitors back to colonial times. The **Smithville Inn** has been serving diners since 1787. You can kick back with a hot cup of coffee or you can shop 'til you drop, whatever your preference. There are 40 shops and boutiques, including the Christmas Shoppe, Cook's Corner, and the Candle Shoppe. There's even an Italian/American novelty store. During the year, Smithville plays hosts to various events, which have included both an Irish and an Italian festival, Oktoberfest, and a Corvette show.

Lucy the Elephant (all ages)

9200 Atlantic Ave., Margate; (609) 823-6473; lucytheelephant.org. Open Wed through Fri from 11 a.m. to 4 p.m., Sat and Sun from 10 a.m. to 5 p.m.; closed Mon and Tues. Admission costs $7 for adults, $4 for children ages 2 to 12, and free for children under 2.
A 65-foot tall wooden elephant, Lucy is older than the Statue of Liberty and was built as a publicity stunt. James V. Lafferty had the idea for an animal-shaped building and even applied for a patent that suggested the structure would be anything but an elephant. Somehow, Lucy ended up being just that. Lafferty's goal was to attract real estate to his property in what is today Margate. Lucy was built in

Devil **in the Details**

One of New Jersey's most famous residents is the **Jersey Devil,** who has been living in the Pinelands for more than 250 years. Even today, people report seeing the Devil, which has the head of a dog, face of a horse, and the body of a kangaroo with wings, horns, and a tail. The story goes that a woman who lived in Estellville was expecting her 13th child and cried out in anger, "Let him be the devil." When he was born, he was indeed the Jersey Devil and flew into the nearby swamp immediately after being born. Since then, he travels around southern New Jersey both terrifying and enthralling people. The story of the Jersey Devil—and the legends surrounding him—make for great campfire fodder. And he's so famous that the state's hockey team, the New Jersey Devils, has taken him as its name and mascot.

1881 for a reported $25,000, which was astronomical for the time. But, thanks to her height, she caught the eye of a young seaman and then the newspapers. The publicity intrigued people, who started coming to check out the pachyderm. Today you can still visit Lucy and take a tour of her insides, which includes stairs in her legs and the floor and rooms in her belly.

Noyes Museum of Art (ages 6 and up)

733 Lily Lake, Oceanville; (609) 652-8848; noyesmuseum.org. Open Mon through Sun from 10 a.m. to 4:30 p.m., Thurs until 8 p.m., and Sun from noon to 5 p.m.; closed for holidays. Admission costs $5 for adults, $4 for students and seniors (ages 65 and up), free for children ages 6 and under.

This is your chance to expose your children to the arts. Born in 1983 from the vision of Fred W. and Ethel (Lingelbach) Noyes Jr., the museum displays fine and folk art from the 19th to 21st centuries. Among the exhibits is Fred's artwork and his collection of vintage bird decoys. The Edwin B. Forsythe National Wildlife Refuge is located next door. The view and the art come together to inspire.

Storybook Land (all ages)

6415 Black Horse Pike, Routes 40/322, Egg Harbor Township; (609) 646-0103 ext.
5; storybookland.com. Open year-round. Admission costs $21.95 for each child or
adult.

Visitors to Storybook Land say it is as manicured and polished as Disney World,
and its offerings bring children's treasured storybooks to life. Family-friendly
rides include the Tick-Tock Clock Drop, Beanstalk Bounce, and J&J Railroad. You
can pass by Mother Goose on your way to Cinderella's pumpkin carriage and
Alice's Wonderland. Little Red Riding Hood and Hey Diddle Diddle are others you
might encounter along the way. A happy hayride and Christmas lights parade are
examples of special seasonal events you might catch, depending on when you
visit.

Wetlands Institute (all ages)

1075 Stone Harbor Blvd., Stone Harbor; (609) 368-1211; wetlandsinstitute.org.
Open in the summer Mon through Sat from 9:30 a.m. to 4:30 p.m., with special
evening hours (until 8 p.m.) on Tues, Wed, and Thurs, and Sun from 10 a.m. to 4
p.m. Open in the winter Tues through Sat 9:30 a.m. to 4:30 p.m.; closed Sun and
Mon. Admission costs $8 for adults ages 12 and up, and $6 for children ages 2
to 11.

For the last 40 years, the Wetlands Institute has promoted the sustainability of
healthy wetlands and coastal ecosystems. An English cottage garden designed
to attract birds and butterflies welcomes guests to the institute. The Salt Marsh
Trail brings visitors up close and personal with fiddler crabs, birds, and other
wildlife. Anyone who wants to get a view of the Jersey Shore—from Sea Isle City
to Wildwood—won't want to miss the Observation Tower. From 40 feet above
the ground, you can take in the view of the wetlands, too. In the winter, visitors
can take self-guided tours of the grounds. In the summer, they can participate
in a guided tour, boat rides, kayaking, live animal shows, and guided beach and
dune walks.

Where to Eat

Borgata Buffet. 1 Borgata Way, Atlantic City; (609) 317-1000; theborgata.com. All-
you-can-eat buffet gives your family many options, and you're certain to find something for everyone. $$$

Harrah's Waterfront Buffet. 777 Harrah's Blvd., Atlantic City; (800) 645-6774; harrahsresort.com. Open Sun from 9 a.m. to 10 p.m., Mon from noon to 10 p.m., Tues and Wed from 4 to 10 p.m., Thurs from noon to 10 p.m., Fri from 4 to 10 p.m. and Sat from 9 a.m. to 10 p.m. This buffet is fabulous because you can have made-to-order pasta dishes and all the crab legs you can eat. $$$

Rainforest Cafe. Trump Plaza, The Boardwalk at Mississippi, Atlantic City; (609) 441-6000; trumpplaza.com. Open for lunch and dinner. Kids will love stepping into the rain forest for a taste of classic children's dishes and fun creatures to entertain them. $$–$$$

White House Sub Shop. 2301 Arctic Ave., Atlantic City; (609) 345-1564. Open daily. This historical sandwich shop is a favorite with celebrities and features fresh baked bread and the finest of ingredients. $$

Where to Stay

Borgata Hotel Casino & Spa. 1 Borgata Way; (609) 317-1000; theborgata.com. This is one of the newest hotels in Atlantic City, and you'll feel like you're living in luxury should you stay there. $$$

Harrah's Atlantic City. 777 Harrah's Blvd., Atlantic City; (800) 645-6774; harrahs resort.com. You'll love the indoor pool that will have you feeling like you are in the tropics, even in winter. $$

Trump Plaza. The Boardwalk at Mississippi, Atlantic City; (609) 441-6000; trump plaza.com. Conveniently located, the Trump Plaza in Atlantic City offers fun for the entire family and is more than just the casino. $–$$

Cape May County

A peninsula and the oldest seashore resort in the US, Cape May County is shrouded in folklore. Rumors have circulated for hundreds of years about Captain Kidd's buried treasure being somewhere in these parts. As a result, people have tried digging up Cape May Point more than once. The county's past as a whaling community has had people wondering if you could really see whales here. At one time, you could. But too many of them were killed, and the residents turned to agriculture to earn a living. Still, the legend of whale sightings lives on. The county came into its own in relatively modern times. By the 1950s and 1960s, the Wildwoods became the place to be during the summer, especially if you were into doo-wop. You can still find remnants of that culture—both in memorabilia and the midcentury-modern architecture—all over the area. With a population of just over 97,000, the county maintains loads of small-town charm. Today visitors come to Cape May County for its beaches, antiques shops, and lighthouses. And the folklore is simply an added bonus.

Cape May County Park & Zoo (all ages)
4 Moore Rd., DN801, Cape May Court House; (609) 465-5271; co.cape-may.nj.us.
Open 10 a.m. to 3:45 p.m. in winter, 10 a.m. to 4:45 p.m. in summer; park is open
from 9 a.m. to dusk. Admission is free for all.
Opened every day except for Christmas and with no admission fees, the Cape May County Park & Zoo is as convenient as it is entertaining. With 550 animals, the zoo delights with giraffes, zebras, tigers, and lions among others. In addition to the zoo, the surrounding park offers playgrounds, picnic areas, fishing ponds, a disc golf course, and paths for walking or bicycling.

Cape May **Beaches**

Cape May has some of the most beautiful beaches in the country. You can opt to check out all of them or pick your favorite and rest there for the duration of your vacation. Here is a list of beaches for you to consider:

The Cove
This beach is perfect for families because the hard sand makes for safe strolls and the ocean waves are fairly calm for swimming. Some people even fish there. Often, you can see dolphins.

Higbee Wildlife Management Area
Secluded Higbee Wildlife Management Area is of great value to endangered, threatened, and nongame wildlife and is the perfect place for a run on the sand with the dog. But insiders say you have to be careful bringing the kids there because it attracts nudists.

Poverty Beach
Poverty Beach is a favorite with locals. Its name comes from the belief that "the help" used to frequent this beach. It is rich with benefits, including showers and free parking.

Sunset Beach
Well known for its sunsets (duh!) and its Cape May diamonds—pure quartz crystals—which wash up on the shore, Sunset Beach is a tranquil setting that offers a bit of romance for the adults in the family and diamond sand for the kids.

Steger's Beach
This is the popular kids' table of beaches. It's where high school kids go to see and be seen. Your preteens might enjoy hanging there. Word is that the food is great, too.

Windsor Beach
Offering visitors the chance to lounge on the sand, Windsor Beach is also an optimal spot for watching schooners and other ships sail by.

Historic Cold Spring Village (all ages)

720 Rte. 9 South, Cape May; (609) 898-2300; hcsv.org. Open year-round. Prices depend on attractions and shops you frequent.

This is your chance to pretend you are living in early America during the 18th and early 19th centuries. You can go from house to house and shop to shop to speak with others from that time. Dressed in period costumes, they will demonstrate everyday tasks. For instance, a basket weaver will teach you her art on the porch at the David Raylor Shop, a housewife will show you how to garden or cook on an open hearth at the Spicer-Leaming House, and a schoolteacher will spend some time explaining a typical day of learning at the Marshallville School. At the Country Store, you can purchase jams and jellies, sweet treats, and wooden toys. Kids will get a kick out of trying on costumes, making handmade crafts, and playing games at the activity area.

Morey's Piers & Beachfront Waterparks

3501 Boardwalk, Wildwood; (609) 522-3900; moreyspiers.com. Open Apr through Oct. Ride and waterpark combo passes offer your best value and cost $225 for a family of four, $64 for those over 54 inches, $61 for those 48 to 54 inches, and $48 for those under 48 inches. There are other prices for just rides or just waterpark admission.

Each of Morey's 3 piers has a distinct personality and offering. Mariner's Landing Pier is traditional with rides like the teacups, the Giant Wheel, and games of luck. Surfside Pier is meant to be a seaside carnival with a mix of grown-up thrill rides and kiddie attractions. Adventure Pier's name says it all; the Grand Prix Raceway, Screamin' Swing, and Snake Slide are for those with no fear, although the carousel is perfect for the kids. The Ocean Oasis Waterpark and Beach Club offers guests the chance to enjoy water rides, rent cabanas, and go to the spa for a massage and other relaxing treatments. For more heart-pounding action, you might head to the Raging Waters Waterpark, which includes a 1,100-foot-long Endless River and a Rope Swing with 10-foot-deep waters for expert swimmers only. There are also family-friendly attractions like an interactive kid's play area.

Where to Eat

The Lobster House. Fisherman's Wharf, Cape May; (609) 884-8296; thelobster house.com. Open Jan through Mar from 11:30 a.m. to 3 p.m. and 4:30 to 9 p.m.; open

Apr through Dec from 11:30 a.m. to 3 p.m. and 4:30 p.m. to 10 p.m. Lobster is not all you will find on this menu. Fresh Jersey clams, oysters Rockefeller, and all sorts of other fish abound. $$–$$$

Mad Batter Restaurant & Bar. 19 Jackson St., Cape May; (609) 884-5970; mad batter.com. Open for breakfast, lunch, and dinner, but check the online calendar for specific hours. The children's menu features three-cheese mac and cheese, flounder, and fun frozen drinks in a variety of flavors. $$

Washington Inn. 801 Washington St., Cape May; (609) 884-5697; washingtoninn .com. Open for dinners Fri and Sat from 5 p.m. Among the top restaurants in the country, this is a must-try menu. $$$

Where to Stay

Congress Hall. 251 Beach Ave., Cape May; (888) 944-1816; congresshall.com. This is an oceanfront hotel resort that will have you feeling rich. $$$

Madison Avenue Beach Club. 605 Madison Ave., Cape May; (888) 884-8266; madisonavenuebeachclub.com. Specials, such as staying for 2 nights and getting 1 free, make this a viable option for families. $–$$

Family-Friendly New Jersey Festivals & Celebrations

The following schedule of festivals and special events is based on plans in place at the time of publication. This is just a small list of our favorites, but check with local websites for more events! Keep in mind that dates are always subject to change, so please call ahead before finalizing your plans.

March/April

Lil' Peep Hayride & Easter Egg Hunt. Mullica Hill; (856) 881-6800; mullicahill .com. Come meet the Easter Bunny, take a hayride, play games, and meet the barnyard pets.

April

Cherry Blossom Festival. Branch Brook Park, Newark; (973) 268-2300; branch brookpark.org. An annual celebration of the park's 2,000-plus cherry trees. When in bloom, they dress the park like pink snow.

Spring Plant Sale & Earth Day Celebration. Layton Road, Far Hills; (908) 234-2677; somersetcountyparks.org. The event takes place at the Leonard J. Buck Garden and features speakers and guided tours of the grounds.

Fun in **Hoboken!**

Hoboken is crazy for parades and festivals! There are countless fairs, holiday celebrations, and even baby and pet parades! Check out hobokenmuseum.org/events/calendar-of-events for a complete list of Hoboken-hosted events throughout the year.

May

Spirit of the Jerseys State History Fair. Washington Crossing State Park, Titusville; state.nj.us/dep/parksandforests. Now is your chance to spin wool on a spinning wheel and participate in a Revolutionary War military drill.

Family Fun Day. Lord Stirling Stable, Basking Ridge; (908) 766-5955; somerset countyparks.org. An annual event since 1981, the festival involves pony rides, tractors pulling wagons for hayrides, arcade games, face painting, and other family activities.

June

Annual Rose Day. Colonial Park, Franklin Township; somersetcountyparks .org. The celebration of peak bloom at the Rudolph W. van der Goot Rose Garden dates to 1974. The garden displays more than 3,000 roses in hundreds of varieties.

Whitesbog Blueberry Festival. Browns Mills; whitesbog.org. Historic Whitesbog Village in the Brendan T. Bryne State Forest is the birthplace of the cultivated blueberry, which is New Jersey's official state fruit. Elizabeth White gets credit for persevering when those all around her had eyes only for cranberries.

Red, White & Blueberry Festival. Hammonton; hammontonnj.us. This annual tribute to New Jersey's official state fruit features music, crafts, food, a display of classic cars, and amusement rides.

State Fair Meadowlands. Meadowlands Sports Complex, East Rutherford; njfair.com. This family-oriented event runs for more than 2 weeks.

July

Oceanfest. Long Branch. An all-day event on the Fourth of July, held every year since 1990, that incorporates crafting, sand sculpture, food vendors, dancing, music, carnival acts, and clowns.

Feast of St. Ann. Hoboken. This is an Italian festival with time on its side and authenticity to back it up. Dating to 1910, it runs for several days and nights, and the food is superb.

New Jersey Sand Castle Competition. 18th Avenue Beach, Belmar; njsand castle.com. This down-the-Shore annual event has been drawing entrants and spectators for a quarter of a century. These castle-dreamers' masterpieces take up about 5 blocks.

Kaboom! Fireworks on the Navesink. Red Bank; kaboomfireworks.org. Held every July 3 for more than half a century, this burst of drama takes place at River-side Gardens Park.

New Jersey State Ice Cream Festival. Downtown, Toms River; (732) 341-8738; downtowntomsriver.com/icecream. Families come in droves for the games, rides, food, and entertainment.

Native American Festival. Sussex County Fairgrounds, Augusta. This event features songs, food, crafts, and art.

Quick Chek New Jersey Festival of Ballooning. 39 Thor Solberg Rd. (Solberg Airport), Readington; (800) 468-2479; balloonfestival.com. This annual up-and-away dates to the 1980s. You can reserve a sunrise balloon ride, or be a specta-tor at dawn and dusk ascensions. Traffic tends to build up around 4:30 p.m. on Saturday, so to avoid traffic, plan to arrive a bit earlier. You will have time to walk the festival grounds, enjoy the crafters and vendors, and scout the entertain-ment. This is the largest summertime hot-air balloon and music festival in North

America. Here you will see more than 100 sport and novelty hot-air balloons from around the world. The event lasts for 3 days, draws more than 165,000 people, and raises money for charities. You can go up, up, and away, or simply marvel at the color-splashed skies. There are live concert series featuring top entertainers, fireworks, a nighttime balloon glow, aerial performers and other attractions, the "Running with the Balloons" 5K Race and Family Fun Run, children's amusement rides, interactive exhibits, arts and crafts, and food vendors.

Warren County Farmer's Fair. Harmony Township (north of Phillipsburg); warrencountyfarmersfair.org. The fair got official in the 1930s but began in the 19th century when farmers planned family get-togethers. In 2000 the event added a hot-air balloon festival into the 8-day mix. There is food, entertainment, and displays of vintage cars.

August

Thunder Over the Boardwalk. Atlantic City; atlanticcitynj.com/acairshow. This perennial crowd-pleaser features the precision skills of pilots with the US Air Force, Army, Navy, the Coast Guard, and the Canadian Skyhawks parachute team.

New Jersey State Fair/Sussex County Farm & Horse Show. Augusta; newjerseystatefair.org. The state fair is chock full of fun events and highlights include a milking contest and livestock exhibitions.

LBI Longboard Classic. Ship Bottom, Long Beach Island; livingocean.org. This event toasts the legendary surfboard and incorporates an environmental fair.

September

Feast of the Madonna Dei Martiri. Hoboken; hobokenitalianfestival.com. This cultural festival dates to the 1920s. It goes on for days, featuring food, music, and fireworks.

John Basilone Parade. Raritan; basiloneparade.com. This annual tribute recalls the heroism of Raritan-native John Basilone, a US Marine Corps gunnery sergeant who was killed at the Battle of Iwo Jima during World War II. This happened after he had received the Medal of Honor for heroic service in the Army. He was heralded in a homecoming parade in 1943 and later reenlisted in the Marines.

Peters Valley Fine Craft Fair. Layton; (973) 948-5200; petersvalley.org. The Peters Valley Craft Center is your host, and its annual fair has been a tradition since 1970. There are even fun art activities for the kids.

Annual Giant Craft Show. Central Avenue and Ocean Pathway, Ocean Grove; oceangrove.org. This event has taken place every Labor Day weekend since 1981.

Island Beach State Park Beach Plum Festival. South Seaside Park; (732) 793-5525; friendsofislandbeach.com. This celebration of the resource takes place at Ocean Beach Swimming Area No. 1; there is beach-plum picking and jelly making, bird-banding demonstrations, exhibits by environmental and non-profit groups, arts and crafts, children's games, a kayak raffle, food, and live entertainment.

Ship Bottom Irish Festival. 10th Street and Shore Avenue, Ship Bottom, Long Beach Island; (609) 494-6301; lbiaoh.com/ifest. Hibernians, and those who wish they were, gather each year at the Ship Bottom Boat Ramp Parking Lot.

The Red Bank Guinness Oyster Festival. RiverCenter, Red Bank; onlyonered bank.com. This street festival is patterned after the Galway Oyster Festival, which has a 60-year tradition. There are 2 stages, food, and music, from Irish folk to blues, funk, and rock 'n' roll, plus children's activities. Red Bank restaurants participate in this fund-raiser.

October

Arts & Main Fall Festival Street Fair. Grove to Doughty Street, Somerville; findsomerville.com. Music, crafts, and artists cause a stir downtown.

Halloween at Batsto Village. Batsto Village, Hammonton; batstovillage.org. Fun annual event for children 12 and younger (with parents) held on the Sunday before Halloween.

The Lord Stirling 1770s Festival. Basking Ridge; somersetcountyparks.org. The manor estate and grounds of Lord Stirling take on a colonial atmosphere, with pre-Revolutionary crafters and a militia conducting maneuvers.

Chowderfest Weekend. Ship Bottom, Long Beach Island; visitlbiregion.com. The chow-down follows the annual showdown as entrants compete for the best New England and Manhattan-style clam chowders.

The Country Living Fair. Batsto Village, Hammonton; batstovillage.com. Crafts, exhibits, music, old-time engines and cars, food, antiques, pony rides, farm equipment, chain-saw art, and quilting.

December

Annual Gingerbread Wonderland. Frelinghuysen Arboretum, 353 E. Hanover Ave., Morris Township; (973) 326-7601. An annual exhibit of 200 edible "structures." The event coincides with a Holiday Craft Show, where you can find hand-made holiday gifts.

First Night. Red Bank; new-jersey-leisure-guide.com/red-bank.html. Held on New Year's Eve in numerous locations around the US, this art and entertainment festival celebrates alternatives to alcohol-related events.

Index

Already "Been There, Done That"
Then Get Off the Beaten Path!

OFF THE BEATEN PATH®

A GUIDE TO UNIQUE PLACES ➡

"For the traveler who enjoys the special, the unusual,
and the unexpected."—*The Traveler* newsletter

Alabama	Kansas	New Hampshire	Rhode Island
Alaska	Kentucky	New Jersey	South Carolina
Arizona	Louisiana	New Mexico	Southern California
Arkansas	Maine	Metro New York	Tennessee
British Columbia	Maritime Provinces	Upstate New York	Texas
Colorado	Maryland & Delaware	North Carolina	Utah
Connecticut	Massachusetts	Northern California	Vermont
Dakotas	Michigan	Ohio	Virginia
Florida	Minnesota	Oklahoma	Washington, D.C.
Georgia	Mississippi	Oregon	West Virginia
Hawaii	Missouri	Pennsylvania	Wisconsin
Idaho	Montana	Philadelphia	Wyoming
Indiana	Nebraska	Puerto Rico	
Iowa	Nevada	Quebec	